Twayne's United States Authors Series

Sylvia E. Bowman, *Editor*

INDIANA UNIVERSITY

Mother Butler Library
Marymount Manhattan College
221 East 71st Street N. Y. 21

**A million candles have burned
themselves out.   Still I read on.
—Montresor.**

ROBERT EMMET SHERWOOD

By R. BAIRD SHUMAN
Duke University

COLLEGE & UNIVERSITY PRESS · *Publishers*
NEW HAVEN, CONN.

Distributed by
GROSSET & DUNLAP
NEW YORK

This COLLEGE AND UNIVERSITY PRESS *edition*
is published by Special Arrangement
with TWAYNE PUBLISHERS, INC.

Library of Congress Catalog Card Number: 64-13954

MANUFACTURED IN THE UNITED STATES OF AMERICA BY
UNITED PRINTING SERVICES, INC.
NEW HAVEN, CONN.

Par 11.95 8/6/66

For the quick and the dead:

DAVID HUNT, M. D.
and
GORDON EDWARD BAIRD
1927-1949

Preface

IN 1936 GRENVILLE VERNON wrote in *Commonweal* (Vol. XXIII, p. 664): "Unlike most Broadway playwrights, Mr. Sherwood has both beliefs and feelings, and unlike the propaganda brethren, he has a subtle mind and a sensitivity of impression which makes him at home in the region of the ironic." Sherwood's subtle mind and his urbanity combined to make him one of the most appealing and popular playwrights of the American theater from 1926 until 1941. Sherwood, sensitive to the intellectual and social currents which affected his age, often wrote of these currents with the extreme irony which pervades a play such as *The Petrified Forest* in which the accepted codes of morality—as represented by the Chisholms, Boze, and the American Legion—are portrayed as being false and, in the latter case, even dangerous standards; whereas the standards subscribed to by Duke Mantee and Alan Squier have an attractiveness and vigor. In this respect, one can certainly compare *The Petrified Forest* with scores of social dramas which were to appear on Broadway at about the same time: *Street Scene, Johnny Johnson, Awake and Sing!, Paradise Lost, Our Town, Winterset, Strange Interlude, Mourning Becomes Electra,* and a host of others.

The present study is concerned largely with evaluating a major portion of Sherwood's literary production. His juvenile works are not discussed due partly to their inaccessibility and partly to the space limitations of this study. The writer has not been able to examine a complete and authoritative manuscript of Sherwood's pacifist play, *Acropolis,* which was performed briefly on the London stage in 1933, but which neither played on Broadway nor was published. Hence it is not fully discussed here.

Sherwood's adaptation of Jacques Deval's *Tovarich* has not been discussed in detail, nor has Philip Barry's *Second Threshold,* for which Sherwood wrote the ending after Barry's death. Neither of these plays reveals much about Sherwood's literary development that would be relevant to the present study. *Miss Liberty*, a collaborative effort, is also excluded from extensive discussion because it is of less direct pertinence than the plays which have been considered. For similar reasons, Sherwood's dramatization of Ring Lardner's *The Love Nest* is given only brief mention.

The organization of the book is thematic in a rather broad sense. The development within each chapter is essentially chronological. An exception to this occurs in Chapter 4 where *The Virtuous Knight* is discussed last because it is a novel, as opposed to the plays dealt with in the chapter. Specifically, biographical consideration of Robert Sherwood has been limited to the first chapter and is presented primarily as the author's life relates to his works. A thoroughgoing biography of Sherwood, soon to be published by John Mason Brown, will be much fuller in detail than any biographical consideration could be in the present volume.

Sherwood's overall development follows a curious pattern. He began his Broadway career in 1926 with *The Road to Rome* which was an immediate success. He struggled through the production of three plays and one novel before he was able to approximate the success of his first major production with the presentation in 1932 of *Reunion in Vienna*. Between 1932 and 1940, his only commercial failure was *Acropolis*. However, as Sherwood became more and more involved in his work with the Playwrights' Producing Company, the American National Theatre and Academy, the Office of War Information, and the Roosevelt administration, his writing suffered a marked decline. His sentiments regarding pacifism were to undergo a severe change with the rise of Nazism in Germany; and, as international circumstances forced him to take stands which he could not comfortably take, he became increasingly ineffective in his dramatic writing. He was writing of ideas, and after 1939 history began to force upon him ideas which he could not easily accept.

Sherwood's work with the Hopkins papers consumed a great deal of his time in the years immediately after the close of World War II. In writing the voluminous *Roosevelt and Hopkins*, Sherwood finally had an opportunity to follow his natural penchant towards historical writing. Since this book is not essentially literary, it is excluded from the present discussion.

It is significant to note, however, that *Roosevelt and Hopkins* provided Sherwood with a form of escape at a time when he much needed it. The war had left a profound mark upon his thinking; he had come to question the validity of his cherished beliefs which had been given full expression in *The Road to Rome, The Petrified Forest,* and *Idiot's Delight.*

The beginning of his disenchantment can be seen in *Abe Lincoln in Illinois* and is much more fully expressed in *There Shall Be No Night. The Rugged Path* is a weak play largely because Sherwood was writing about the disenchantment but was, at the same time, idealistically trying to fight it. The result is that the thinking in *The Rugged Path* is not clear. Sherwood escapes from the horns of his dilemma in this play by having the protagonist, Morey Vinion, go to war as a means of personal escape rather than as a result of personal conviction. The hints that the personal conviction is also present are always overshadowed by the obvious fact that Morey Vinion is running from a way of life repugnant to him. In *The Road to Rome,* Hannibal yields to the force of words and ideas as well as to the charms of Amytis. But Morey Vinion abandons faith in words, which he as a journalist must have, in favor of direct action in combat against the forces opposing democratic existence. However, Sherwood seems to experience a sense of guilt in presenting Morey Vinion in purely idealistic terms, and he assuages this guilt by making excuses for his idealistic protagonist. This salve to the author's conscience is poison to the dramatic possibilities of his play. Turning to *Roosevelt and Hopkins* enabled Sherwood to deal with objective fact rather than with personally painful ideology.

American drama has been born in a period of profound social dislocation. There was little noteworthy American drama before World War I, for even O'Neill's most significant works came after 1918. The reaction of playwrights to the social dislocation of their age has been diverse. The propagandists and the specifically proletarian playwrights wrote vigorously about causes and often used the stage as an oversized soapbox. But Sherwood generally dealt with more abstract material than did the proletarian writers; and his urbanity prevented him from being a soapbox orator, even though an occasional speech in some of his plays approaches such oratory.

Sherwood's contribution to American theater was not made as playwright alone. His leadership in the founding of the Playwrights' Producing Company and his presidency of the American National Theatre and Academy redounded to the benefit of an enormous number of people directly concerned with the theater.

This book represents the first full-length critical-analytical study of Robert Sherwood. Happily, it will be followed by Mr. Brown's biography. The serious student of Robert Sherwood's contribution to American theater would also do well to consult Paul Charles Harris's fine unpublished doctoral study of Sherwood which is noted in the bibliography.

R. BAIRD SHUMAN

Ensenada, Mexico
28 March 1963

Acknowledgments

For their inestimable help and encouragement to the author during the preparation of this book grateful acknowledgment is made to the following people:

H. Charles Hutchings, II, of the University of California at Los Angeles, who read and made valuable comments about the entire typescript.

Sylvia E. Bowman, who edited the typescript speedily, intelligently, and understandingly.

Mrs. Edwin C. Bolles of Carmel, California, and Zdenek I. Vana of San Francisco, who offered suggestions on Chapter I.

Hector Lopez y Meza of Ensenada, Mexico, who helped the author through the stages of preparing the final draft.

Mrs. Mary Cheatham of Duke University, who prepared the typescript.

Mrs. Spears Hicks of the Duke University Library, who was indefatigable in tracking down obscure sources.

William H. Cartwright, Chairman of the Department of Education, Duke University, for his understanding when research and writing interfered with the author's participation in departmental routine.

Paul and Elizabeth Green of Chapel Hill, who were valuable sounding boards for some of the author's ideas enunciated herein.

The Duke University Council on Research for giving generous financial aid to the writer while he was pursuing this study.

Elizabeth T. Gwin and Arthur Bliss Perry of the Milton Academy, who provided the author with information about Sherwood's student life at the school.

The following are commended for having permitted the author to use quotations from sources on which they control the copyright:

The Catholic University of America Press for permission to quote from *Politics in the American Drama* by Casper Nannes, © 1960.

Contents

Chronology

1896　Robert Emmet Sherwood is born in New Rochelle, New York, on April 4.

1903　Edits small, family-produced magazine called *Children's Life*.

1904　Plans a revision of *Tale of Two Cities*: attempts to write an ending to *Edwin Drood*.

1906　Writes first play, *Tom Ruggles' Surprise*.

1909-　Attends Milton Academy.
1914

1912,　Spends his first summer in Britain.

1914　Enters Harvard University, begins contributing pieces to *Vanity Fair* under his own name and under the pseudonym Brighton Perry.

1917　Writes *Barnum Was Right* for Harvard's Hasty Pudding Club; editor of Harvard *Lampoon*; leaves Harvard when the United States enters World War I; joins the Canadian Black Watch Regiment after he is rejected for service in the United States Army and Navy because he is too tall.

1918　Serves with Black Watch Regiment in Britain and France; gassed at Vimy Ridge; returns to active duty and is shot in both legs at Amiens; spends remainder of war in British hospital at Bushy Park outside of London; Harvard awards him Bachelor of Arts degree.

1919　Released from hospital; returns to United States; is employed by *Vanity Fair*, but he and Robert Benchley resign when Dorothy Parker is dismissed from the magazine; goes to Boston to supervise Hasty Pudding production of his *Barnum Was Right*, an earlier production of which had been postponed because of the war.

1920　Takes job as feature writer for Boston *Post*, but is fired after two days.

1920- Employed by *Life* in various capacities; writes first
1928 United States film reviews in 1920, and by 1923 is called
dean of American motion-picture critics; becomes editor
of *Life* in 1924; is fired in 1928 because he is obdurate in
his opposition to Prohibition and to Herbert Hoover.

1922 Marries Mary Brandon on October 29; writes *The Dawn Man* which is never produced.

1927* *The Road to Rome* is produced; *The Love Nest* is produced.

1928 *The Queen's Husband* is produced.

1930 *Waterloo Bridge* is produced; *This Is New York* is produced.

1931 *The Virtuous Knight* is published.

1932 *Reunion in Vienna* is produced; buys farm at Great Enton, Surrey, England.

1933 *Acropolis* produced in London; *Reunion in Vienna* made into film.

1934 Divorces Mary Brandon Sherwood.

1935 Marries Madeline Hurlock Connelly on June 15; becomes secretary of Dramatists' Guild; *Petrified Forest* is produced.

1936 *Idiot's Delight* is produced and wins Pulitzer Prize; Sherwood's adaptation of Jacques Deval's *Tovarich* is produced; writes scenario for *The Ghost Goes West*; *Petrified Forest* made into film.

1937 Becomes president of the Dramatists' Guild; becomes a founding member, with Maxwell Anderson, S. N. Behrman, and Elmer Rice, of the Playwrights' Producing Company; writes scenario for *Thunder in the City*.

1938 *Abe Lincoln in Illinois* is produced; writes scenario for *The Adventures of Marco Polo*.

1939 Receives Pulitzer Prize for *Abe Lincoln in Illinois*; hears William L. White's Christmas broadcast from Finland entitled *Christmas in the Mannerheim Line* and starts to

* In the case of Sherwood's major dramas, the date ascribed is that of the first Broadway performance.

write *There Shall Be No Night* based on the Finnish plight; *Idiot's Delight* made into film; *Abe Lincoln in Illinois* also made into film.

1940   Appointed special assistant to the Secretary of War; awarded Doctor of Literature by Dartmouth College; *There Shall Be No Night* is produced; *Waterloo Bridge* made into film; becomes president of American National Theatre and Academy (ANTA).

1941   Receives the Gold Medal for Drama of the National Institute of Arts and Letters; awarded Doctor of Literature by Yale University; receives his third Pulitzer Prize for *There Shall Be No Night.*

1942   Appointed director of the Overseas Branch of the Office of War Information.

1943   Revised edition of *There Shall Be No Night* appears; Greece is substituted for the now subjugated Finland.

1944   Resigns as director of the Overseas Branch of the Office of War Information.

1945   Appointed special assistant to the Secretary of the Navy; *The Rugged Path* is produced.

1946   Writes film play *The Best Years of Our Lives* which wins nine Academy Awards.

1948   *Roosevelt and Hopkins* is published.

1949   Awarded Doctor of Literature by Harvard; for his *Roosevelt and Hopkins* he becomes the first recipient of the Gutenberg Award and also receives his fourth Pulitzer Prize and the Bancroft Prize for Distinguished Writings in American History; *Miss Liberty* is produced.

1950   Awarded Doctor of Civil Laws by Bishop's University; revised edition of *Roosevelt and Hopkins.*

1954   Signs contract with the National Broadcasting Company to write nine television plays over a period of five years.

1955   Dies on the morning of November 14.

1957   *Small War on Murray Hill* is produced.

CHAPTER 1

Another Hungry Gulliver

I *Six Foot Seven*

THE INGENIOUS and provocative title which Pamela Hansford Johnson chose in 1947 for her study of Thomas Wolfe —*The Hungry Gulliver*—is as descriptive of Robert Emmet Sherwood as it is of Wolfe. Physically, Sherwood and Wolfe were of almost equal height, although the six-foot-seven inch Sherwood was of a somewhat leaner frame than Wolfe. Intellectually, the title is equally applicable to both: each had an insatiable intellectual curiosity which motivated in each a wide variety of interests and activities. Wolfe was writer, teacher, indefatigable traveler, violent liver of life, mercurial, brilliant, often wide-eyed; Sherwood was writer, presidential advisor, casual wanderer, quiet savant, saturnine, unobtrusively intelligent, often painfully shy.

The first meeting with Sherwood might have led one to think that this towering man was comfortable only when alone. Conversation with him was discomfiting to those who did not know him well, for great hiatuses occurred between every syllable he uttered. When he attended dinner parties, he often found himself utterly deserted: people on both sides of him would turn to their companions on the other side to avoid having to engage in conversation with one whose speech was so painfully deliberate. The story is now legendary that George Bernard Shaw, when he was host at a London dinner party at which Sherwood was present, attempted to draw the lanky playwright into the conversation by discoursing with typical Shavian fluency and animation on nineteenth-century liberalism. Sherwood's attention apparently was more on his dinner than on Shaw's conversation, for, when Shaw suddenly turned his attention upon Sherwood and asked, "Don't you agree with me, Mr. Sherwood?", Sherwood swallowed magisterially, glanced about the table, fixed his eyes finally upon Shaw, gathered his verbal forces about him, and with slow deliberation asked Shaw what he had said. Shaw repeated his question. Another prolonged silence ensued as the assembled guests awaited the utterance which appeared to be rising from the depths of Sherwood's deeply intellectual soul. His moustache moved almost imperceptibly. His lips parted. With the grandeur of a bishop reciting the Miserere on Ash Wednesday, he answered, "Yes. I agree with you." With that utterance, he gave everyone leave to return to the important and immediate task of completing his meal.

Despite his natural reticence and the lugubriousness of his plodding speech—a lugubriousness which once prompted Noel Coward to ask Sherwood's sister, "What is this nine foot tower of gloom you call your brother?"—Sherwood was able to gain mastery in social situations when he desired to do so. John Gassner very perceptively indicated this ability in Sherwood when he wrote, "In the theatre he is not only one of the masters of his craft, but the one playwright in the lobby or in the haunts of the after-theater set who overshadows celebrities of the acting profession without so much as a word on his part to call attention to himself."[1] It was not entirely Sherwood's towering body that accounted for this impressiveness. It was more his warm sincerity, his casual gentility, his restrained but obvious brilliance which caused him to be noticed and to be honored by those who fell under his spell. And among those who came to have a profound appreciation for Sherwood were such notables as Franklin Delano Roosevelt, Harry Hopkins, Winston Churchill, Maxwell Anderson, Elmer Rice, B. Charney Vladeck, Elmer Davis, Archibald MacLeish, S. N. Behrman, and a legion of other dignitaries from all walks of life.

II *Thoroughly Tired of Grandpa*

Perhaps Robert Sherwood grew into a quiet, meditative man because he had exhausted the outward manifestations of his exuberance in childhood. A lineal descendant of Robert Emmet, a heroic and martyred defender of Irish freedom, Sherwood gave early evidence that Irish blood was surging through his veins. He tormented an incapacitated grandmother by urging noxious insects in her direction. When he was seven, he was left to spend the summer with his grandfather while his mother and sister Cynthia vacationed in Europe. In his grandfather's house was one of the modern miracles of plumbing, a flush toilet. Sherwood's grandfather was expansive with pride when he heard the water from this innovation cascading through the newly installed pipes within the walls of his comfortable house. Sherwood, even then disdainful of pride in anyone, decided to reduce his grandfather to a state of utter humility. He accomplished this by dumping the toy animals from his Noah's Ark into the toilet and pulling the chain. Shortly thereafter the malfunctioning of the equipment was noted, and the plumber who had installed it was summoned and thoroughly castigated. He apologetically set to work to repair the plumbing. Moments later he retrieved a wooden elephant which he held up triumphantly saying, "It's a good closet, but you can't expect it to pass elephants." At the conclusion of what to Sherwood and his grandfather must have seemed an interminable summer, young Robert greeted his mother by saying, "I am thoroughly tired of Grandpa." Grandpa's remarks when Robert departed are not recorded.

These events took place in the summer of 1903, just one hundred years after Thomas Addis Emmet, expelled from his native Ireland, had come to the United States where he established the American branch of the Emmet family and where he soon gained for himself a most favorable reputation as an attorney. This branch of the family has produced many notable offspring; among them are Sherwood's uncle, William LeRoy Emmet, one of the greatest American engineers, winner of an Edison medal in science, and successor to Steinmetz in the General Electric research laboratories; and Sherwood's mother, the former Rosina Emmet, whose distinction as an artist won her a place in *Who's Who* long before her son had made his mark as a dramatist. For five successive generations the Emmet family has produced artists of note.

Sherwood's father, Arthur Murray Sherwood, was a successful investment broker and a member of the New York Stock Exchange. Throughout his life he was a frustrated thespian who, because of his great height, had been dissuaded in his youth from seeking a career on the stage. As a student at Harvard he was active in the Hasty Pudding Club, and he was the founder and first president of the *Lampoon*. Today in the office of the *Lampoon* can be seen a plaque given by Arthur Murray Sherwood whose name is inscribed upon it above the words "First President." One of the great and memorable occasions of the elder Sherwood's life came when he was admitted to membership in the Lamb's Club.

When Sherwood was only seven, he edited a small magazine called *Children's Life*. A year later he planned a revision of *A Tale of Two Cities,* and he attempted to write an ending for Dickens' unfinished novel, *Edwin Drood.* He wrote his first play, *Tom Ruggles' Surprise,* in his tenth year. At an early age he was a discriminating reader and showed an especial preference for reading works dealing with history. When the Sherwoods summered on Lake Champlain, Robert frequently wrote, directed, and acted in amateur theatrical performances with his brothers and sisters and with any neighboring children who might be available. The cast sometimes outnumbered the audience by four or five to one, but Sherwood was never daunted by this great disbalance.

As Robert approached high school age, his parents thought it best for him to attend private school and to live away from home. He was sent to Milton Academy in Massachusetts and was there prepared for his ultimate matriculation at Harvard. While at Milton, he is said to have fought heroically to quell a fire in one of the school buildings. He later confessed to his brother that he had started the fire on an impulse.[2]

In 1914 when he was eighteen years old, Robert Sherwood entered Harvard University where his unrestrained *joie de vivre* brought him to the brink of expulsion on three separate occasions during his freshman year. However, he soon found constructive ways in which to sublimate his high spirits. As an upperclassman he was a key member of the Hasty Pudding Club for which he wrote a play, *Barnum Was Right*; and, following in his father's footsteps, he was editor of the *Lampoon*. It was during his tenure as editor that the *Lampoon* did its now famous burlesque on *Vanity Fair,* a burlesque which so greatly impressed *Vanity Fair's* editor, Frank Crowninshield, that he promptly offered

Sherwood a position on the magazine as soon as he was graduated.

However, World War I intervened; and, when America entered the conflict in 1917, Sherwood left Harvard to serve his country. He attempted to enlist first in the United States Army, and then in the Navy. Both of these services rejected him on account of his prodigious height, whereupon Sherwood went to Montreal and joined the 42nd Battalion, Black Watch, of the Canadian Expeditionary Force. Sherwood had the singular honor of being the tallest service man to wear kilts through the first global conflict. So tall was Sherwood that, when a photographer tried to photograph him in his kilts, he found it impossible to have both the head and the legs in focus simultaneously. Hence, the pictures which Sherwood's family had taken of him showed the granite-like Emmet features with great clarity, but showed his legs only as long, fuzzy vertical structures.

Sherwood's unit was first shipped to England and in 1918 saw combat in France. He was gassed at Vimy Ridge, but recovered sufficiently to return to combat and to participate in the defense of Arras and Amiens before he was wounded in both legs and hospitalized initially in Amiens and then later at Bushy Park outside of London.[3] Although he was an ambulatory case during most of his time at Bushy Park, his hospitalization was not officially terminated until January, 1919, after which he was honorably discharged from the armed services and returned to the United States.

The effect of the war upon the young soldier was profound. Eager to fight for democracy in the early stages of the conflict, he was soon to admit that he had hoped he would be hospitalized until hostilities ceased. His pacifist philosophy began to emerge while he was a soldier in France. It grew increasingly as he witnessed the horrors resulting from war during his confinement in the British hospital. Specific incidents from this confinement give rise to the whole of *Waterloo Bridge* and to parts of Sherwood's novel *The Virtuous Knight*. But the total experience served to mold the young man's thinking and to make itself felt directly in such plays as *The Road to Rome* and *Idiot's Delight,* in a more indirect and philosophical way in *Abe Lincoln in Illinois,* and in a more highly developed and indeed more pessimistic way in *There Shall Be No Night.*

Sherwood's boyhood ended sometime during his first year at Harvard. He was easing his way into manhood when he was forced to exchange the security of the campus for the hell of the battlefield; and, on the battlefield, he was suddenly catapulted into manhood amidst the unrelenting diapason of war. The searching youth who had left Boston in 1917 returned to New York in 1919, having been brushed by eternity. The memory of his experiences was sharply with him, and the first significant ingredient of his major dramas was now his. He was at this point on the threshold of gaining the second significant ingredient.

III *Mr. Editor*

Upon his return to the United States, Sherwood was told by doctors that his heart had been affected when he was gassed at Vimy Ridge and that his life expectancy was not great. They recommended that he lead a very relaxed life in the hope that he might survive somewhat longer by assuming the role of a semi-invalid. Sherwood thought semi-invalidism a complete bore and did not even submit to a week of it on a trial basis. Rather he plunged into a very demanding position as a literary jack-of-all-trades for *Vanity Fair*. He soon became master of the glib line and the hasty rewrite. Since his work was largely to bolster the sagging prose of *Vanity Fair* contributors, much of the writing he did was fragmentary and, of course, anonymous. His subjects ranged from golf to gardening, from badminton to *belles lettres*.

During the war, while Sherwood was abroad with the Black Watch, his father had suffered a breakdown in his health as well as a serious decline in his fortunes. It was, therefore, vital that Sherwood earn enough, at least, to be self-supporting. The position at *Vanity Fair* assured him of enough income to maintain himself, but not enough for him to live very lavishly or to be able to put money aside. He enjoyed the variety of his work, and he was pleased with the thought that through it he was being schooled in professional writing. However, his ire was evoked when the editor of *Vanity Fair* dismissed Dorothy Parker because she had written some mildly caustic theatrical reviews; and, although he could ill afford to take a moral stand over this dismissal, Sherwood promptly resigned from *Vanity*

Fair—as did Robert Benchley. Having very little money and no job, Sherwood was delighted to accept the invitation of the Hasty Pudding Club to come to Cambridge and direct the production of his play written while he was in college, *Barnum Was Right*, the original production of which had been postponed when America entered the war.

Living an economically perilous existence in Cambridge, Sherwood acceded very happily to Neal O'Hara's request that he become a feature writer for the Boston *Post*. This position was terminated abruptly at the end of its second day because Sherwood had let his sense of whimsy overcome his adherence to truth in reporting the opinions of the Dean of Women at Boston University whom he had interviewed on the subject of premarital sexual relations. Fortunately for both the Boston *Post* and Sherwood, this interview was never published. Sherwood, again jobless, returned to New York.

After a period of searching, Sherwood, through the efforts of his father's old friend, E. S. Martin, then one of the editors of the old *Life,* secured a position on this magazine which was originally an outgrowth of the *Lampoon*. During the same week, *Life* hired Robert Benchley and Dorothy Parker and the warm friendship which had begun on *Vanity Fair* continued for nearly a decade as the three worked closely together on *Life*.

Sherwood's earliest significant job on *Life* was that of associate editor in charge of motion-picture criticism. In 1920 there were few motion-picture critics and those who were writing did little more than present plot summaries; however, Sherwood reviewed films critically in terms of the writing, direction, production, and acting. By 1923 his reputation was established in the area of motion-picture criticism, and he was writing reviews for the New York *Herald, McCall's, Photoplay*, and other magazines. He received up to three hundred dollars for a single review. A large part of his life during this period was spent in darkened cinema houses and in the taxicabs which transported him from theater to theater. He had little time for the pursuit of his favorite pastime, the reading of history. However, his eminence as a motion-picture critic resulted in his being elevated in 1924 to the editorship of *Life* with the understanding that he would continue to be a motion-picture critic for the publication.

During his second year at *Life,* on October 29, 1922, Sherwood was married to Mary Brandon of Indianapolis. One child, Mary, was born of this union: the marriage ended, however, in 1934 when Sherwood divorced his wife. It was also during his time at *Life* that Sherwood was to meet and establish a lifelong friendship with Sidney Howard. Emotionally and spiritually akin, their affinity to each other was immediate. Through Howard, Sherwood was to become concerned with the relationship of theater to the community; later Howard was to convince Sherwood of the need for theatrical people to band together into groups or unions which would fight for and protect their interests.

Many people felt that Sherwood and other movie critics were perpetrating and perpetuating some sort of intellectual and artistic fraud by giving serious consideration to motion pictures, a relatively new medium. Sherwood felt that he was somewhat ostracized for championing silent films until such actors as Charlie Chaplin, Ernst Lubitsch, Erich von Stroheim, and Douglas Fairbanks, Sr., made them more respectable. He freely admitted that, while the motion picture might be used ". . . for the dissemination of distasteful junk, it may also be used for the dissemination of ideas that are beautiful and important."[4] Further, he considered the motion picture ". . . an honest medium through which an artist may express himself intelligibly, eloquently and effectively."[5] He looked upon motion pictures more as a challenge to legitimate theater than as a threat to it. He wrote that "The future of the theatre depends on one consideration: its ability to give its audiences something which they can't obtain, more cheaply and more conveniently, in the neighboring cinema palaces."[6] He welcomed the advent of talking pictures because they forced directors to plan scenes in advance and they tended ". . . to shake the non-gifted out of Hollywood."

As early as 1929, Sherwood publicly discussed the possible effects of television upon the world of entertainment. He predicted that it would be upon the scene within five years and that with it would come an enormous increase in general advertising. He felt that two types of theater would remain— those showing high-level, limited-appeal films and plays; and cheap theater catering to those who did not have television. He contended that "The theatre is an impractical institution in this age of transportation and communication. Its chief purpose has been to provide refuge and diversion and distraction for those dwellers in cities and towns who were stifled by the narrowness of their own homes. The automobile has made it easy for such people to break away. . . ."[7]

Chronologically, Sherwood was a member of that generation which Gertrude Stein had designated as "lost." But Sherwood was not lost, at least not in the way that Gertrude Stein had in mind when she created her memorable label. Sherwood had returned from his war experience with the perfect rationalization for being lost—his doctor's gloomy diagnosis. Despite it, he had established firm roots in the magazine business, become a respected critic and respectable citizen, and risen to a position of importance in his profession. Nevertheless, he had been swept up to some extent by the extravagant living of the 1920's; and, by 1926, he found himself sufficiently in debt to need some extraordinary means of lightening his financial burdens.

It is not surprising that he should find the answer in the writing of plays: he had studied dramatic technique thoroughly as a part of his work as critic; he had become a glib and easy writer; as an amateur, he had gained experience in both the writing and directing of plays; he was well enough grounded in history that he had ready subjects about which to write; and he had a definite pacifist philosophy which he wished to air. Besides these assets, as Eleanor Flexner indicates in her *American Playwrights, 1918-1938,* "The revival of Shaw's *Caesar and Cleopatra* several seasons before, the fad for historical novels couched in an irreverent modern idiom, had paved the way for a similar development in the theatre of which *The Road to Rome,* in 1927, was the first successful native example."[8]

Sherwood's *The Road to Rome,* his first professional play, was immediately rejected by Gilbert Miller with the comment that he didn't ". . . even like *first-rate* Shaw," and the play was, indeed, constantly compared to Shaw's play which had modern themes in classical settings. *The Road to Rome* was readily accepted for production by Brady and Wiman and—with Jane Cowl and Philip Merivale in the roles of Amytis and Hannibal, respectively—became a rousing success on broadway. Sherwood's financial problems were solved, and he could easily have turned his back on the editorship of *Life.* However, he remained with the magazine until he was forced to leave it in 1928 because of his vehement stands against Prohibition and against Herbert Hoover. It was in the decade after he had left *Life* that Robert Sherwood was to make his most significant literary contributions, and it is doubtful that he would have been able to make them had he continued to be concerned with the routine problems that daily face an editor.

In 1928, then, it may be said that the second literarily significant period in Sherwood's life had closed, just as in 1919 the first had ended. Now he had had the experience of war, from which had emerged his strong pacifist feelings, and the experience of working in a variety of journalistic jobs, from which had emerged the literary skill and acumen he was to employ so effectively during the next major period of his life—the period of his emergence as a significant, recognized, and highly successful playwright.

IV *Hokum of the Highest Type*

Webster's Dictionary identifies *hokum* as a slang noun which in a play or in speech indicates the deliberate stimulation of emotion by artificial means. The term has often been applied to Robert E. Sherwood. Euphemia V. R. Wyatt claimed that he had ". . . a good sense of honest hokkum [*sic*]";[9] and a writer for *Time Magazine* contended that "Hokum of the highest type has long been the priceless stock-in-trade of Robert E. Sherwood."[10] Sherwood, who was always a dispassionate critic of his own work, in retrospect, at least, would have been the last to deny these judgments. He often spoke harshly of his plays. He contended, for example, that *The Road to Rome* ". . . employs the cheapest sort of device—making historical characters use modern slang."

Eleanor Flexner noted that in many of his plays Sherwood used ". . . a background of war or violence which endangers the lives of his characters. This is Sherwood's device for sustaining tension, a device forced upon him by his inability to construct a play in which suspense will arise from the actions of the characters themselves."[11] Actually this perceptive statement indicates in large part a reason for the frequent "hokum" in Sherwood's plays.

In 1927, the same year in which *The Road to Rome* was produced, Sherwood's *The Love Nest,* a play based on a Ring Lardner short story, was produced on Broadway. This play, trivial and often inept, collapsed with an appalling thud. Sherwood was not to produce another play to equal the popularity of *The Road to Rome* until his production in 1932 of a comedy in the continental tradition, *Reunion in Vienna.* Meanwhile, he was to write three other plays and a novel, all of little significance. He found himself constantly overshadowed by his first play, and it appeared at times that he would never again reach the level which he had achieved so gracefully in *The Road to Rome.*

The Queen's Husband, an ephemeral little piece produced in 1928, was primarily a jibe at Marie Alexandra Victoria, Queen of Rumania from 1914 to 1927,[12] who in 1926 paid a state visit to the United States. This play was followed in 1930 by the somewhat subjective play, *Waterloo Bridge,* the artistic caliber of which exceeds that of *The Queen's Husband. This Is New York,* a somewhat inchoate piece mildly suggestive of *The Petrified Forest,* was produced in the same year. In 1931, Sherwood's only novel, *The Virtuous Knight,* was published by Charles Scribner's Sons. Neither the three plays nor the novel can be termed successful either artistically or commercially. The best of the lot was *Waterloo Bridge,* but it certainly did not measure up to *The Road to Rome;* nor did it suggest the potential which Sherwood was to show in such plays as *Reunion in Vienna, Idiot's Delight, The Petrified Forest, Abe Lincoln in Illinois,* or *There Shall Be No Night.*

In 1929, Sherwood visited Europe for the first time since his return from the war. *The Road to Rome* was opening in Vienna, and the author attended the opening night. Afterwards he and his party took a droshky down the Opernring to the Hotel Sacher off the Kärtnerstrasse. The party was greeted by Frau Anna Sacher who, in the manner of Danish women, had taken to smoking great fat cigars. Old Frau Sacher took an immediate liking to Sherwood and showed him through the famed hotel, delighting him with such items as the white damask signature tablecloth, signed by over 140 highly distinguished guests through the years and carefully embroidered by Frau Sacher herself. He was shown the menu which Crown Prince Rudolf had himself written out only days before his tragic death in 1889 at his hunting lodge in Mayerling. But what impressed Sherwood most was seeing the ornate Baroque room, which Frau Sacher had reserved for parties given by one-time Austrian aristocrats whose fortunes were depleted but whose pride and memories remained. This room represented to Sherwood the desperate attempt of a people to cling to the past in the face of cataclysmic change. Frau Sacher was sentimental about this room, and her sentimentality was subtly transmitted to Sherwood who never quite forgot the room and all that it implied and whose sentimentality about it grew through the years.

Back in New York in 1931, Sherwood, who liked to work in offices amid much noise and confusion, sat at his desk in the office building of Charles Scribner's Sons on Fifth Avenue and was again haunted by the thought of what he had seen at the Hotel Sacher two years earlier. He began to write, and within three weeks he had completed *Reunion in Vienna*. The play, produced in 1932 in both New York and London starring Alfred Lunt and Lynn Fontanne, was even more successful than *The Road to Rome* had been. The film rights were sold for $85,000, and Sherwood's star was distinctly in the ascendant.

Sherwood and his wife were in Hollywood in 1932 when they had the opportunity to buy a farm at Great Enton in Surrey. Sherwood felt that it would be well for them to spend their summers in England away from the pressures of New York and Hollywood; so, he bought this farm where he spent most of his summers until the war intervened just after he had returned to the United States at the close of the summer of 1939. The farm then became a refuge for children who had to be evacuated from London.

In 1934, Sherwood went to Reno to obtain a divorce from his wife. He had been there only two or three days when he rented an office and began writing a play. This play was to be set in the general area of Reno and was, as it turned out, Sherwood's most allegorical production. A nostalgic kind of play, it bared the quintessential emotions of characters who were removed from their own social contexts. In a sense it is suggestive of plays such as Sir James Barrie's *The Admirable Crichton*. However, it has in it the distinct appeal of sensitive, esthetically aware youth in the person of Gabby, about whom much of the play revolves.

Sherwood completed this play two weeks before the requisite six, sent it off to New York, and confessed that ". . . the last two weeks were terribly boring." The play opened at Hartford shortly before Christmas, 1934, and began its New York run in the first week of 1935. A commercial and artistic success, its dependence upon "hokum" is readily discernible. Sherwood was fortunate that the mood of 1934-35 provided a receptive audience for this rather fanciful play which he was able to sell to Hollywood almost immediately for $110,000. It was the sort of thoughtful escape drama which made it possible for playgoers to forget their own immediate depression problems without being plagued by guilt at escaping into revelry.

In 1935, Sherwood went to Europe and there married Marc Connelly's former wife, Madeline Hurlock Connelly. During this trip to Europe, Sherwood observed characters with whom to people his next play; moreover he made mental notes and mulled over what he wished to accomplish in his next production. In the same year Sherwood became intensely interested in the Dramatists' Guild of which Sidney Howard was president; Sherwood became secretary of this organization.

Still disappointed by the failure of his play *Acropolis,* an anti-war drama which had died after a short run in London in 1933, Sherwood was determined to produce another play which would serve as a vehicle for his pacifist sentiments. Finally after returning to the States, Sherwood settled down to writing a new anti-war play. He remained in his apartment in New York for the better part of two weeks during which he worked through many nights, unable to sleep because his mind remained active with ideas for the play long after he had retired. At the end of two weeks he had written *Idiot's Delight* and had sent it to the Lunts for a reading. The play, produced on Broadway in 1936, won for its author his first of four Pulitzer Prizes. The film rights brought him $135,000. During the same year, his adaptation of Jacques Deval's *Tovarich* was produced, *The Petrified Forest* was released as a film, and Sherwood wrote the scenario for the motion picture *The Ghost Goes West.*

Sherwood was becoming increasingly interested in finding means for protecting the rights of actors and authors in the legitimate theater, and in 1937 his interests led him first to become president of the Dramatists' Guild, and then—with

Maxwell Anderson, S. N. Behrman, and Elmer Rice—to become one of the founders of the Playwrights' Producing Company, an organization designed not only to give the playwright a greater return from productions of his plays, but also to give him more of a voice in their production. The first play scheduled for production by the Playwrights' Producing Company was the highly successful *Abe Lincoln in Illinois* on which Sherwood had been working when the company was organized. During 1937 he completed last-minute work on the scenario of *Thunder in the City*, and, once this was done, he pushed ahead on *Abe Lincoln in Illinois* which was first presented in 1938 and which won the 1939 Pulitzer Prize in drama. The film *The Adventures of Marco Polo* for which Sherwood did the scenario was also released in 1938.

Both *Idiot's Delight* and *Abe Lincoln in Illinois* were made into films in 1939. Sherwood received $225,000 for the film rights to the Lincoln play, and was to receive also a share of the profits. The world was apprehensive in 1939, and Sherwood probably knew when he summered in England that it was unlikely he would be there again for some time. He spent many of his days lazily, breakfasting late, reading his papers, placing bets on the horses which he followed daily when in England. Sherwood suffered through the events of September, 1939; he wanted to help but was not entirely sure how he might best do so. His philosophy was changing from one of outright pacifism to one which stressed the necessity for stopping the advance of the Axis powers. As his philosophy changed thus, it became clear that his pacifism had been essentially an emotional rather than an intellectual reaction to the problem of human conflict.

Sherwood was ostensibly at work during this period rewriting *Acropolis* for the Lunts. He spoke little of what he was doing, but he had promised the Lunts and the Playwrights' Producing Company that he would rework this play for presentation sometime in the near future. His work was not progressing well. On Christmas day, having heard William L. White's broadcast from Finland entitled *Christmas in the Mannerheim Line*, he set to work making notes about the Finnish situation. On January 15, 1940, he began writing a play about the plight of the Finns, and twenty-six days later he gave the typescript of *There Shall Be No Night* to the Lunts who were on the brink of departure for their Wisconsin farm. Lynn Fontanne read the play on the train and wired Sherwood from Chicago that she would act in it. Shortly thereafter, another wire from Chicago announced that Alfred Lunt would play Dr. Valkonen. The play opened in Providence, Rhode Island, on March 29, 1940; and it had a highly successful, extremely controversial Broadway run. The play was rewritten in 1943, after the Finns had been conquered, and the Greeks became the oppressed people represented in it.

With the onset of the war, Sherwood came full circle in his thinking. The motives which had impelled him to leave Harvard and join the Black Watch in 1917 were now strong in him again. He wished to join the army or navy, but when he realized that he would not have an active role in the conflict, he rejected this idea. He expressed his philosophy regarding the war against the Axis in *There Shall Be No Night*. He was now to turn to more active war work, and this work constitutes the next major period of his life.

V *State of Tremblage*

Sherwood had known Franklin Delano Roosevelt in the 1920's; and, when Roosevelt became the standard bearer of the Democratic Party in 1932, Sherwood was vigorous in his support of Roosevelt's presidential candidacy. Jubilant at the Democratic victory, Sherwood set to work writing a lengthy poem for the inauguration. Like most occasional pieces, this poem[13] entitled "Inaugural Parade" was a rather tired piece. Sherwood's strong pacifist propensities were the chief motivating forces behind the sentiment in these verses which borrowed heavily and consciously from the national store of patriotic verse and which employed catalogues and slang usage to achieve the atmosphere suggestive of an expansive democracy. However, the poem was insightful in some respects as the following lines attest:

> Some licking lips at the prospects for theft—
> Others, it seems, in a great state of tremblage
> Lest this procession should turn to the left.

The poem ends with the plea "God save our planet."

Inferior though this poem obviously is, it is historically significant in that it marks the beginning of an official relationship between Roosevelt and Sherwood. Sherwood was to be one of Roosevelt's major speech writers during the years to come and was frequently a guest at the White House. The President, who had great admiration for Sherwood, found in his quiet self-assurance a source of strength in trying times. He unofficially sought Sherwood's cool-headed advice on affairs of state, and the two often talked far into the night for the sheer pleasure of each other's company.

In 1940, before the United States had entered the war, Roosevelt appointed Sherwood special assistant to the Secretary of War. Many people who had called *There Shall Be No Night* a war mongering piece of propaganda felt that this appointment was a fitting step on Roosevelt's part. Actually, Sherwood did not give an inordinate amount of his time to the War Department for he was much involved in the business of running the American National Theatre and Academy (ANTA) of which he was president. However, it was definitely rumored that Sherwood was slated for appointment to a top government post, and in 1941 the news leaked out that he was to replace Joseph Kennedy as Ambassador to Great Britain. Both Sherwood and the government promptly denied this rumor, and it is now evident that it was actually nothing more than a rumor.

Shortly after the entry of the United States into the war, Sherwood was appointed director of the Overseas Branch of the Office of War Information, then run by Elmer Davis. He served for nearly three years in this capacity before resigning late in 1944. His work was primarily concerned with establishing short-wave radio stations, dropping leaflets on Germany, and supplying information to the subjugated people of France to arouse them to action against their oppressors. In this position he was responsible for the direction of one-thousand eight-hundred government employees and for the expenditure of annual appropriations of between $20 and $30 million.[14]

Sherwood was serving most effectively in a very sensitive and important position, but he was becoming less and less the playwright as he increasingly became involved in government. It can be said unqualifiedly that he never achieved another artistic stage success after *There Shall Be No Night*. His only productions for the legitimate stage after the war were *The Rugged Path* which was on Broadway in 1945 and *Small War on Murray Hill* which was produced in 1957, two years after Sherwood's death.

In 1949 Sherwood completed *Second Threshold*—a play that death prevented its author, Philip Barry, from completing—which was rather poorly received. Also in 1949, Sherwood collaborated with Irving Berlin and Moss Hart on a musical comedy, *Miss Liberty*. He undertook this collaboration as a rest from the labors involved in writing his compendious historical volume, *Roosevelt and Hopkins* which, among other things, was a distillation of forty filing cabinets full of Hopkins' papers to which Sherwood had unlimited access.

The greatest triumphs in the last decade of Robert Sherwood's life came in 1946 when he won an Academy Award for his scenario, *The Best Years of Our Lives,* a film which received eight other Academy Awards. In 1949, *Roosevelt and Hopkins* brought him the first Gutenberg Award ever granted, the Pulitzer Prize for writings in history, and the Bancroft Prize for Distinguished Writings in American History. In the same year Harvard awarded him the honorary degree of doctor of letters.

Sherwood's entry into television writing occurred two years before his death. In 1953 he signed a contract with the National Broadcasting Company promising to deliver nine television shows between then and 1958. The first of these shows, *The Backbone of America,* was produced early in 1954. Sherwood had said that "TV is far and away the most difficult medium to write for, because of the terrific precision of the timing."[15] In the same interview he had said that if *The Backbone of America* were a flop, it would be his own fault. The production was generally conceded to have been a complete flop. Robert L. Shayon, writing for *Saturday Review,* entitled his article "Mr. Sherwood in the Wilderness," and lamented that in this new medium Sherwood ". . . stumbled and was bruised." He went on to say that Sherwood writes condescendingly to his audience, and he decried the fact that NBC's contract called for eight more shows.[16] But Sherwood did not live to fulfill the terms of his contract. He died quietly on the morning of November 14, 1955.

CHAPTER 2

Alpha and Omega

". . . there's a thing called the human equation. It's so much more beautiful than war."
— *The Road to Rome*

THERE IS A SINGULAR correspondence between *The Road to Rome*, Robert Sherwood's first Broadway production, and *Small War on Murray Hill*, his last. Both of these plays are concerned with war, and in both the outcome of the struggle is altered through the amorous intervention of a woman of high position. Both plays are indirectly concerned with contemporary conditions and problems, although one is set in the Rome of Fabius Maximus and the other in the New York of General Washington and General Putnam. The protagonists in both plays, Amytis and Mary Murray, are reputedly clever women married to men less clever than themselves. In both plays Robert Sherwood makes dramatic use of history, distorting it to meet his dramatic needs, but he maintains enough historically valid material to place his plays in a convincing historical context. He has been castigated by some purists for the liberties which he has taken with history, especially in *The Road to Rome*;[1] however, his introduction to *The Road to Rome* indicates very clearly what he intends in this play, and he makes no pretense of being historically accurate in his conclusions. Indeed, from the extant materials on Hannibal, even the professional historian can do no more than speculate about why the indefatigable Carthaginian commander turned from Rome when his conquest of the city was a ninety-nine per cent certainty.

Despite the significant points of correspondence between *The Road to Rome* and *Small War on Murray Hill*, the former was a marked success on Broadway and the latter was a total failure. This difference in reception was due in large part to the fact that Sherwood's Hannibal was a commander of infinitely more stature than Sherwood's Howe. His Amytis constantly demonstrated her cleverness, whereas his Mary Murray did not demonstrate hers; instead the audience, told that she is clever, is expected to believe she is. Further, the conquest of Rome constituted the fruition of Hannibal's lifetime effort, while General Howe is depicted—and quite accurately in terms of history—as having serious reservations about the role which England was playing in the American Revolution.

In *The Road to Rome,* as will be shown, the subplot contributes to the development of the play; but in *Small War on Murray Hill* the corresponding subplot is constantly in the way and does nothing to promote the development of the main action. Finally, it is clear that Amytis was a delightful and convincing seductress, enchanting to audiences as well as to Hannibal; but Mary Murray, despite the charms attributed to her in the notations to the play, never succeeds in being anything but a rather pedestrian *hausfrau* who stuffs General Howe with steamed clams and wearily yields to his somewhat uninspired advances. She is never convincing as a charmer or as a seductress. Whereas *The Road to Rome* is a rollicking satire, *Small War on Murray Hill* is a banal, sadly unwitty farce.

I   The Road to Rome

More than two decades after he wrote *The Road to Rome,* Robert Sherwood was to call the play "knee-pants drama" and was to censure himself severely for having used the cheapest of theatrical techniques—introducing current slang into a historical play—to achieve his effects.[2] Actually, Mr. Sherwood dealt more severely with *The Road to Rome* than most critics. Shortly after the play opened for its highly successful London run—one which began, incidentally, after *The Road to Rome* had played 440 times to packed houses in New York—J. T. Grein, writing in the London *Illustrated News,* gave Sherwood the benefit of the doubt and claimed that the colloquialism of the play as well as ". . . the stereotyped figures of the popular 'problem' play—the misunderstood, childless wife; the self-complacent, ineffective husband; the doting mother, jealous of the younger woman's wifehood; the *blasé* yet immature officer brother, 'out to kill' " are employed by the author ". . . with *malice prépense,* his avowed object being the creation of a commonplace background to his story."[3]

Although *The Road to Rome* has some severe technical flaws, the popularity of the play is undeniable. The characterization is superb, the plot construction is generally well planned, much of the humor is appealingly sophisticated—the dependence upon modern colloquialism notwithstanding—the element of irony is very well handled, and the dialogue, though occasionally overburdened with philosophizing, is usually sprightly and spirited. The major flaw—aside from the jarring use of slang in such passages as ". . . don't you litter up this place with no orange peels, neither"[*] (73) or "I don't do no turn with no elephants, see?" (74)—is that the basic theme of the play is obscured by the heavy emphasis which Sherwood places upon the theme of pacifism in the second and third acts.[4]

Actually, pacifism should be a secondary theme in the play rather than the main one. As the action is developed, the main theme, and the real point of the play, is presented through Amytis who asks Hannibal of his four years of conquest, "Why have you done it?" (112). Hannibal has no real answer and from this point forth he comes increasingly to acknowledge by deed, and finally consciously by word (176), ". . . that there's a thing called the human equation" (132). Amytis personifies this theme; her every act reinforces it. And by the time the play nears its end, Hannibal's actions prove that he has grown in his understanding and that, having been touched by "the human equation," he comes to exemplify it in turning Amytis back to her husband in such a way that her association with the enemy remains their secret. However, as the dialogue is increasingly diluted with speeches about the futility of war, the main theme is driven into the background and ultimately is subordinated to the pacifist monologues. The whole broad idea of the potency of words and of human reasoning, an idea strong in the heritage of the Athenians from whom Amytis is a descendant, is made

[*]All references are to the first edition of the play (New York: Charles Scribner's Sons, 1927).

distinctly secondary to the narrower, more specific theme of pacifism.

According to Sherwood's account of his writing of *The Road to Rome*, the play was undertaken after the author had read in Franklin P. Adams' column ". . . that all young newspapermen promise themselves that they will write that play or that novel before they're thirty and then the next thing they know they're forty and still promising." Sherwood did not know what sort of playwright he wished to be, "So I tried in it [*The Road to Rome*] every style of dramaturgy—high comedy, low comedy, melodrama, romance (both sacred and profane), hard-boiled realism, beautiful writing—and, of course, I inserted a 'message.' That message was that I was opposed to war."[5] It is apparent in this statement, written fourteen years after *The Road to Rome*, that Sherwood had by this time ceased to acknowledge what his fundamental theme in the play had been.

The characterization in *The Road to Rome* is well handled and is generally convincing. The play belongs primarily to Amytis and secondarily to Hannibal; however, the supporting characters are well drawn and give strength and dimension to the production. Amytis is married to Fabius Maximus, a Roman senator who has just been named dictator of Rome. Hannibal is camped outside the gates of the city, certain to attack and certain to conquer. Fabius and his mother, Fabia, are representative of the narrow and insular viewpoint which the Romans of that period held. Amytis, on the other hand, represents the wit and intelligence of Athens, inherited presumably from her Athenian mother.

Early in the play the audience is told by Fabius that today the Senate ". . . took constructive, intelligent measures to combat the Carthaginian menace" (15). In short, they appointed Fabius dictator. Fabia, victim to the universal motherly weakness of parental pride, feeds her son's ego so that, by the time Amytis makes her entrance, Fabius is swollen with the feeling of self-importance. Amytis, in the face of a Carthaginian invasion, has been out shopping because there is in Rome a merchant recently arrived from Antioch. Her mother-in-law, already annoyed that Amytis behaves more like an Athenian than like a Roman, greets her by saying, "Amytis, your husband has some great news for you" (21). But Amytis turns a deaf ear to this and babbles on excitedly about her purchases, a Phoenician nightgown from the Court of Antiochus the Great and a peacock-green silk dress from Damascus. After many attempts to tell Amytis the news of the honor bestowed upon her husband, Fabia blurts out triumphantly: "To-day the Roman Senate proclaimed your husband, Fabius Maximus, Dictator." Fabius confirms this with, "Yes, my dear, they have placed me at the head of the Roman state," to which Amytis replies, "Isn't that nice. . . . Tanus, put those things in my room. Go on with dinner. I'll be right back" (22-33). Fabia archly reminds her son that "After all, she's only a Greek."

Fabius, a typical politician, is much concerned with conventional propriety. He reproved Amytis when she used the word "concubine" before the servants. He wonders whether the peacock-green silk dress is ". . . quite the sort of thing to be worn by a lady of your position?" (22). When Amytis suggests going to the theater to see *Oedipus Rex* because "I love to cry. I like to go into the theater and just sob" (29), Fabius responds, "To tell you the truth, Amytis, I've never seen the play—but I've heard that it's—well, that it's rather questionable." Fabia through all of this dotes on her son's conservatism, for it reflects her own narrowness and confirms that her bourgeois attitudes are right.

Amytis, on the other hand, maintains an open mind and feigns ignorance when it is to her advantage to do so. She cleverly says, "Everyone seems to be talking about Hannibal these days, and I'm sick and tired of the sound of his name. . . . By the way, who is he?" (24). Fabius, dumbfounded, chides Amytis for her ignorance, to which she answers: "Why should I know anything about Hannibal? Remember, you confessed to me the other day that you had never heard of Aristotle." Fabius replies: "That's quite true, my dear. But, after all, you must admit that Aristotle never did anything to make himself famous" (34).

In the first act the groundwork is well set for what is to happen. The pace is leisurely throughout the act, but the points of reference are well established. Amytis, in feigned ignorance, makes statements which border on sedition. She says, for instance, "I've heard that Carthage is a very beautiful city"(25). Fabius states his creed when he lists as the more desirable virtues ". . . respectability, modesty, economy, devotion to duty, reverence, chastity, and—and . . ." to which Amytis adds "Mediocrity!" (33).

Amytis is beautiful and charming. Her husband sees little in her beyond this. Her wit is an embarrassment to him; her iconoclasm, an absolute horror. He and Fabia hold her intelligence quite generally in low esteem; Fabius feeds his ego by assuming an understanding attitude toward Amytis. He is a martyr to love; he is convinced that he has married someone who is not his equal. He tries to instruct her in the mores of Rome, mores of which his mother, who calls *Oedipus Rex* "Probably one of the coarsest plays ever written!" (29), is a sterling example.

When it becomes evident that Rome is to be sacked by Hannibal within a matter of hours, Amytis decides to flee to Ostia with her two faithful Sicilian slaves, Meta and Varius. Fabia is horrified, but not surprised that her daughter-in-law should decline to remain in Rome to die heroically beside her husband. Fabius tries to defend Amytis when Fabia turns upon her, but even he becomes visibly annoyed at her indifference to Rome's plight. She leaves, but not before she has suggested that Fabius and his senators try to reason with Hannibal under the flag of truce. Her parting words are "Good-bye, my husband. Don't eat too much starchy food while I'm away" (64).

In this first act, Amytis' method of argumentation is shown very well. It is exasperating to try to argue or to reason with Amytis because she makes argument impossible. When Fabia very nastily says, "You never take the trouble to order the meals," Amytis can only reply very ingenuously, "I'm no good at housekeeping" (30). There are many instances in this act of Amytis' resorting to this technique. Also in this act Amytis suggests what she really is, and heightens the irony of the events when she says, "Perhaps my Athenian frivolousness is purely superficial. Perhaps, in the depths of my soul, I am a stern, relentless, world-beating Roman!" (26). All of this, of course, is in direct preparation for her encounter with Hannibal. The irony in the last sentence of this statement is apparent; it leaves no doubt that Amytis has motives other than a desire to save Rome when she risks her life by going into the camp of the enemy. She has already shown an active interest in Hannibal by the middle of the first act when she says, "You say he is cruel. . . . He sounds like a thoroughly commendable person. . . . Is it wrong for me to admire good, old-fashioned virility in men?" (35).

And she follows this last utterance with a statement which indicates that her marriage to Fabius is not altogether happy: "I certainly haven't seen any too much of it in my own life."

Eleanor Flexner has noted that "The fact that Amytis is not primarily actuated by a desire to save Rome, which she heartily dislikes, but rather by a desire to learn the secret of Hannibal's power and then destroy it, is typical of Sherwood's unromantic romanticism."[6] One might question whether Amytis wishes to destroy Hannibal's power. She admires it enormously, and she wishes to pit herself singly against it. The first part of Miss Flexner's statement, however, is undeniable.

Part of Amytis' strength is her extremely realistic view of life and its situations. She is a complete rationalist, one must assume. She shows no homage to the gods of Rome or of her mother's Athens. When Hannibal bombastically proclaims to her that he is pursuing his conquest of Rome because Ba-al has said to him "Go on, Hannibal, go on, with sword and flame, until you have destroyed the glory of Rome" (121), Amytis reduces the argument to dust in an instant by replying, "That wasn't the voice of Ba-al, Hannibal. That was the voice of the shopkeepers in Carthage, who are afraid that Rome will interfere with their trade." Hannibal, like all great men, is the visionary, the dreamer; Amytis, like all significant women, is the counterbalance, the realist. Hannibal is unquestioning in his service to Ba-al, just as Hasdrubal is unquestioning in his service to Hannibal, as is evident in his statement that "I've never disobeyed an order, Hannibal. What's more, when you've given me a command, I've never even stopped to ask why you gave it. I've accepted everything from you, as though it were the word of Ba-al himself" (172). Hannibal has been just as blind in his dogged obedience.

Amytis is surrounded by unquestioning, unreasoning followers of authority. Her husband and mother-in-law condemn Sophocles although they have no first-hand knowledge of his works. Hannibal lives without question the life which he thinks Ba-al has decreed he should live. Both Fabius and Hannibal are slaves to public opinion. Even as a conqueror, Hannibal is concerned with what the Romans will think if he marches into Rome with his elephants painted "every color in the rainbow." He tells Hasdrubal that "We want the Roman citizens to think that we're an army. We mustn't look too much like a circus parade." Amytis is definitely not of a similar mold; because she cares little for public opinion, she is considered dangerous. But she protests, "I'm not dangerous. I'm only real" (120), and she says to Hannibal that he is afraid that she might make him real.

Actually, at this point in the play she is directly involved in doing just that. Every time Hannibal asks Amytis a question, his own doubt underlies the question. When he asks Amytis, "Do you think you can talk me away from Rome?" (122), he is making a subconscious admission that he is weakening and that Amytis *can* do just that. Amytis responds at this point with an answer which bolsters Hannibal's masculine ego—"I don't care *what* happens to Rome. I'm trying to find something in you, something great, something noble, something exciting" (122). And Amytis may well believe that this is what she is seeking; but, like Chaucer's Wife of Bath, what she really desires is mastery.

Her calculated mastery over Fabius has been based upon her frivolousness and her physical charm; her mastery over Hannibal is based upon her keen intellect and her physical charm. And, through Hannibal, she is to gain a dual mastery over Fabius: she is to return to him after he has followed her suggestion that he negotiate reasonably with Hannibal and has been convinced that the suggestion—for which he receives full credit—has succeeded; and she is likely to bear Hannibal's child who will become the son of Rome's first citizen. In a sense she has had her revenge on Fabius, but only she and Hannibal know this. And the final bit of irony is that, through Hannibal, all is forgiven. Amytis, Fabius is told, has stopped in her flight to the safety of Ostia and has come into the enemy camp out of concern for him. If there is any vengeance against Amytis for her deceit, it is in the fact that for the rest of her life she will have to endure listening to Fabius as he makes such pronouncements as "Hannibal, with all his elephants and all his men, could not subdue the high moral purpose of Rome," and "Virtue, my dear, is the one perfect defense against all the evil forces on this earth" (177), and that she will not be permitted to laugh at them.

The subplot involving Amytis' Sicilian slaves, Meta and Varius, is well used by Sherwood. To begin with, the action of the play opens with these two lovers on stage and their plight is soon revealed. They provide the audience with information about Amytis before she makes her appearance, and the audience in this way has come to know that Amytis is not so frivolous as she first appears. Through the two lovers, also, the audience comes to realize that Amytis has a warm humanity about her and that she is not a loyal Roman. The slaves are invaluable in the rapid development of Fabia's character. She surprises them in an embrace and her imperious nature at once comes to the fore—as does her pettiness.

The barren marriage between Fabius and Amytis is sharply contrasted to the apparently hopeless love affair between the two slaves. They have been in love since childhood, but Roman law forbids slaves to marry. The slaves are really the only friends and confidants that Amytis has in Rome. They are utterly loyal to her, and she to them. When Amytis decides to flee Rome, it is clear that she will take her personal slaves with her. It becomes evident, also, that their liberation is at hand. They have already confided to their mistress their desire to escape, and she is quietly sympathetic to this. Ultimately, she prevails upon Hannibal to release the two so that they can return to their native Sicily and marry, and Hannibal accedes to this request.

Actually, the bravest act performed by Amytis while she is in Hannibal's camp is performed when Meta is nearly seduced by a soldier. Amytis, under sentence of death herself, gains immediate command of the situation and with regal bearing defends her slave, reducing her Carthaginian warders to positions of complete servility. So impressive is her display of strength that Hannibal fears her continued presence. He has already rankled under her charge that he is a murderer, and he now vows that he will make this charge good by executing Amytis himself with Mago's sword. As he raises his sword and verges on the point of stabbing Amytis in the heart, she clings to his arms. Hannibal cries, "You're going to die!" (133); and Amytis, her face close to his, responds, "Yes—I'm going to die . . . but not until tomorrow." Hannibal seizes Amytis and kisses her.

Sherwood uses this psychological device again in *Reunion in Vienna*. When the exiled Archduke Rudolf Maximilian meets his former mistress, now married to a Viennese psychoanalyst, he greets her by slapping her face soundly; after this action, they kiss passionately. It has been thought by some that this rather brilliant touch was added to the script of *Reunion in Vienna* at the suggestion of Alfred Lunt, but Lunt denies this, saying, "That piece of business was in the script. Think of his knowing *that*—that shy man!"[7] Surely this early parallel in *The Road to Rome* indicates that Sherwood, though he may have been shy, was perspicacious and psychologically aware.

The Road to Rome, of course, was intended as a commentary on the America of the 1920's. Sherwood justifies his toying with historical fact by saying, "The representation of Rome itself, as it existed under the Republic, is not unjustifiable, for the spirit of Fabius Maximus and his brother boosters has become the spirit of America to-day. History is full of deadly and disturbing parallels and this, it seems to me, is one of the most obvious parallels of all" (Preface, xxxix). Those who had fought in a world conflict in order that an ideal might survive, only to return to an indifferent America, universally shared Amytis' belief which she eloquently expressed upon announcing that she was not going to remain in Rome and be slaughtered. She told Fabius and his infuriated mother: "I may be a traitor to Rome, but I am not a traitor to my own convictions. I didn't start this war. I've never given it my support or encouragement. I have no axe to grind with Hannibal. Why should I sacrifice my life merely because the Roman army has failed to subdue a weaker enemy?" (59).

In a sense the whole question of personal morality versus public morality is at the heart of this play. The play's great irony is that personal morality on the part of Amytis wins the day for Rome; but public morality, of which her husband and mother-in-law are the prime exemplars, receives the credit.

The Road to Rome was so successful with audiences that Sherwood met a severe challenge in attempting to equal it in his later plays; in fact, not until *Reunion in Vienna* did he write another wholly successful drama. Sherwood resolves the problems in *The Road to Rome* by having words win over force. Miss Flexner notes this fact with lamentation when she states that "Hannibal, the man of force and action, is stripped, emasculated, becomes the victim of abstract ideas. Later his [Sherwood's] heroes become so attenuated that action is foreign even to their past. Hannibal's submission to Amytis is the first step on the road to the futility of Alan Squire and Harry Van."[8] But, regardless of one's emotional or intellectual reaction to Sherwood's method of bringing about the resolution of the conflict in *The Road to Rome,* the play is forceful in the presentation of the basic philosophy that man's reason can overcome his brawn. In a world of a debilitated League of Nations, in an America of disillusioned war veterans, in a New York which was seeking frenetic release from the tensions that a world conflict had engendered in its citizens, Sherwood's appealing play gave pause. When the witty lines had become vague memories, audiences still found the philosophy of the play working upon their consciences and leading them to question seriously the validity of human conflict on a world-wide scale.

II Small War on Murray Hill

Just a little more than a year after Robert Sherwood's death in 1955, his last play, *Small War on Murray Hill,* opened at the Ethel Barrymore Theatre in New York. The play ran for little more than a week and the critical consensus was that, despite the high regard in which the memory of Robert Sherwood was held, his final play was a total failure. The only unrestrained enthusiasm was for the sets designed by Boris Aronson, and it was a rare critic, indeed, who did not lavish extensive praise upon these.

The similarities between *The Road to Rome* and *Small War on Murray Hill* have been noted earlier in this chapter and by most reviewers. Thematically the two plays share a close kinship; however, the distance between the Rome of Fabius and the Heights of Inklenberg cannot be measured in terms either of miles or of centuries. Rome and Amytis and Hannibal had an enchantment about them which Inklenberg, Mary Murray, and General Howe did not even roughly approximate. Sherwood's last play deals with a small part of a small encounter in a remote wilderness; his first play deals with the most crucial hours in the life of a monumental, memorable commander who stood on the brink of conquering the most important city of his age.

Small War on Murray Hill suffers significantly from the fact that General Sir William Howe, both in real life and in the play, had no stomach for suppressing the rebellious Americans. He had gone into battle near Boston where the memory of his brother, who had earlier been killed at Ticonderoga, was still revered. He had fought well at Bunker Hill; but, by the time he reached Manhattan, Sir William was much more eager to drink his 1738 Madeira, bathe in hot water, and sleep in a soft bed than he was to pursue General Putnam, who was encamped nearby. He had every reason to believe that Putnam's army had been decimated and that the British forces could overcome the Americans whenever it was convenient for them to do so. Howe's counterpart in *The Road to Rome* was a man who, through a number of years of the utmost trial and hardship, had been impelled onward by the sincere conviction that he was fulfilling the destiny which his god, Ba-al, had decreed for him. He had crossed the Alps with elephants, he had killed some seventy thousand Romans by employing a brilliant trick in the battle at Cannæ, and he had approached the gates of Rome with every possibility of conquering the eternal city. He was, and to this day is, legendary even though he is known only through the historical records which his enemies have left.

Howe, on the other hand, had been merely a competent military man. He had distinguished himself in Wolfe's expedition to Quebec and had commanded his own regiment in the defense of Quebec in 1759-60. Later he was adjutant-general of the force which besieged and captured Havana. Before taking part in the American Revolution, he had been governor of the Isle of Wight for four years and had been a close friend of Benjamin Franklin through whom he had come to sympathize with the American colonists. When he arrived in America, he served under General Gage whom he regarded with the utmost contempt; he served creditably, but without enthusiasm or conviction. Therefore, had Sherwood wished to recreate *The Road to Rome* in an American setting, it would have been necessary for him to fabricate his general totally—and even then it is doubtful that the effect would have been achieved.

Small War on Murray Hill opens badly. Two officers and an orderly occupy the first few minutes of the action. The officers engage in banal, boring chatter which succeeds in doing little other than give the recipe for pemmican and a sketchy summary of the current military situation in the vicinity of New York.

General Howe's entry onto the scene does not improve the situation greatly. He smells the pemmican, sniffs haughtily, and extends his handkerchief so that his orderly can sprinkle it with cologne. One might expect Sherwood's general to engage in no battle more strenuous than a contest of draughts in the game room of his London club.

General Howe's chief military concern at the beginning of the play is not that of overcoming General Putnam, but rather of keeping his Hessian mercenaries under General von Donop from making the conquest without British aid. The mercenaries are eager for a victory because they realize that, with each victory, they will be more in demand and will be able to command higher remuneration from future employers. Von Donop, a very able commander, is much annoyed that Howe will not push on to this certain conquest at once, and he assures Howe that his men can overcome General Putnam without British aid. Howe realizes that this would be difficult to explain in London, and he restrains von Donop.

Mr. Murray appears only briefly in the play, and the audience has little opportunity to form an opinion about him. He is obviously a sound business man and an opportunist. Howe is not concerned about Murray's loyalty, explaining that "Mr. Murray's highest loyalty is to the Bank of England, and we are the defenders of that"* (16). Mr. Murray is older than his wife, and they are apparently childless. Actually, they are very seldom seen together in the course of the play, so their relationship is never made entirely clear. Apparently Murray is not very perceptive in regard to his wife, for he does not realize that her loyalties are with the colonials. And Mary Murray has secrets from her husband, as is made clear when Samuel Judah, the banker, appears briefly on the scene, and she thanks him for not telling her husband about her overdrafts. Judah seems to understand Robert Murray, for he tries to approach him through his wife with an offer to buy the cargoes of two supply ships which Murray has promised to the British. The implication of this offer is that Robert Murray has the reputation of selling to the highest bidder, regardless of the consequences of the sale.

*All references are to the Acting Edition of the play (New York: Dramatists' Play Service, 1957).

The subplot which deals with the puppy-love affair between Frederick Beckenham, one of Howe's lieutenants, and Susan Lindley, Mary Murray's sister, has no organic relationship to the development of the play in terms of plot, characterization, or theme. It is merely a boring, pointless, episodic obstacle to the forward motion of the play. It does not even serve the function of comic relief. If Freddie's growing love for Susan is meant to be an analogy to General Howe's growing love for Mary Murray, the analogy fails; for General Howe does not love Mary: he merely enjoys the respite from war which her home provides him, and he condescends to seduce her probably because he thinks it is expected of him.

Had Sherwood lived to see this play put into production, it is entirely possible that he would have scrapped the Freddie-Susan subplot and that he would have made General Howe more dashing and dedicated than the real general was. He might then have developed Mary more convincingly as the charming, clever patriot that he wanted her to be; he might also have made *her* the seductress that he had created in Amytis in *The Road to Rome*. He would also have had to distort history somewhat to make General Putnam a more formidable enemy than he was represented to be in this play.

Still, however, the basic problems of *Small War on Murray Hill* persist. In *The Road to Rome*, the tension during the second act is very high and it emanates from the action as it unfolds. Amytis is involved in a life-and-death struggle and the whole future of Rome is dependent upon her success. The threat of imminent danger and the love theme intermingle throughout and each enhances the over-all tension. However, the tension in *Small War on Murray Hill* is never developed through the characters. It is supposed to exist in the situation, but even this is not convincing because of the cavalier attitude with which Howe treats the matter of conquering General Putnam. The only real tension which is created is that between Howe and von Donop, and it detracts from the force of the thematic development rather than adding to it. The contention between Howe and von Donop represent another subplot in the play; and this subplot, too, is distracting, although it can be justified somewhat because it is used to illustrate Howe's attitude toward the conflict in which he is engaged. This subplot is troublesome only because it is carried too far and given entirely too much play.

Small War on Murray Hill is very weak in what John Howard Lawson calls "the obligatory scene," the scene which involves a test of strength.[9] There is little evidence that Mary Murray has a moral struggle to overcome before she decides whether to give in to General Howe; and General Howe approaches the seduction of the colonial housewife with a dutiful determination rather than with a suddenly awakened passion. The prelude to their intimacy occurs when Mary gives General Howe a copy of Marivaux's *La Vie de Marianne*. The dialogue which follows the bestowal of this gift is ludicrous:

HOWE. (*Rises, crosses to her.*) I shall carry it in my kit as if you had tossed me your garter from the battlements.
MARY. (*Rises, crosses L. to desk.*) Really, Sir William!
HOWE. Yes, *really*, Mary Murray!
MARY. Isn't our little chat bordering on the indiscreet?
HOWE. What if it is?
MARY. Don't you often think that the cardinal sin is indiscretion? (*Howe looks at her for a moment, closely.*)
HOWE. I seldom burden myself with such discouraging thoughts.
(55-56)

This sort of banter is well suited to a light comedy such as *Lady Windermere's Fan*; in *Small War on Murray Hill*, it is vapid, unconvincing, and defectively epigrammatic. Compare this exchange with those between Amytis and Hannibal, and particularly with the brash, brazen suggestion of the voluptuous Amytis who says to Hannibal, "But no soldier ever kills a woman until he . . . and *especially* if she happens to be attractive" (124).

When Howe finally makes his "proposition," it is hard to tell *what* he is proposing. He asks Mary, "Aren't you going to ask me to stay the night?" (58). She answers, "No," and the dejected Howe says that, if she wishes it, he will go off to sleep on some sack of straw on some windswept hill. The melodrama increases to the point that one begins to disbelieve what he is seeing and hearing. Mary suggests that she may be in the employ of General Washington, to which Howe replies, ". . . if it's true that he has assigned you to this degraded task, then I can only assume that he damned well deserves to win," and so saying he takes Mary, the free-lance patriot, into his arms and kisses her gently. The chop-logic of his final utterance is incredible and really defies analysis.

In his review of the play, Henry Hewes made a sound point when he indicated that General Howe's battle fatigue was soon caught by the entire audience.[10] There was an indisputable lethargy about the play. Perhaps, as Miss Wyatt suggested, the material which Sherwood used was just too thin for a full-length play.[11] She felt that the author had failed to dramatize the very desperate condition of the colonial army and that the play would have been strengthened had he done this.

Time Magazine called the play ". . . too reflective for light comedy, yet . . . not nearly stimulating enough for a comedy of ideas,"[12] and Wolcott Gibbs complained that the humor consisted of ". . . elaborately turned epigrams . . . or else of endless quips about the quaint place names."[13]

One can only assume that the criticism of *Small War on Murray Hill* is essentially criticism of an unfinished, unpolished piece of writing. The play does not seem characteristic of its author who, as Wolcott Gibbs noted in his review of the play, had turned out a dozen plays which, with two or three exceptions, had demonstrated ". . . pace, animation, and considerable skill in theatrical construction."[14]

CHAPTER 3

Sherwood's Universal Microcosms

"Thus in your field my seed of harvestry will thrive —"
— The Petrified Forest

IN *This Is New York, The Petrified Forest,* and *Idiot's Delight,* Robert Sherwood communicates his ideas to his audience by consciously creating a microcosm in which are found representative social prototypes. He uses his microcosm in each of these plays to bring together people who would not normally be found together and who, in some cases, speak for segments of society which are antipodal. In *This Is New York,* for example, an ultra-conservative United States senator and his socially proper wife are drawn by circumstances into a "kept" woman's plush apartment, through which wander a racketeer, two lesbians, a prize fighter, and a judge corrupted by Tammany Hall. In *The Petrified Forest,* a setting removed from the infinite variety of New York, the combinations are even more unlikely, for into the Black Mesa Filling Station and Bar-B-Q come an Ohio banker with his wife and chauffeur, a hitch-hiking writer down on his luck, a puerile football hero, a desperado and his henchmen, and an American Legion Commander. And in *Idiot's Delight* circumstances bring together a ski instructor, the leader and director of a girly show with six of his peroxided beauties, a research physician about to discover a cure for cancer, a honeymooning British couple, an Austrian waiter made Italian by the Treaty of Versailles, a number of Italian officers, a French pacifist, an Italian consumptive and his wife, and a munitions manufacturer and his mistress. In none of his other plays does Sherwood depend so much upon fortuitious circumstance to bring together his spokesmen as he does in the three plays to be considered in this chapter.

These plays cover a time span of six years. *This Is New York* was produced on Broadway in 1930; *The Petrified Forest,* in 1935; and *Idiot's Delight,* in 1936. The first of these plays has received little critical acclaim and, despite very well-written passages within it, is generally a rather defective piece that is interesting primarily because it gives some insight into Sherwood's groping for a method of presentation which he perfected in the latter two plays. In terms of mastery of technique and dynamism of writing, *The Petrified Forest* and *Idiot's Delight* have been regarded by critics as being nearly equal. Both plays were highly successful on Broadway, and later in the films. *Idiot's Delight* won the Pulitzer Prize for Drama in 1936, and *Time Magazine* reported that the awarding of the prize for this year, usually ". . . the subject of violent differences of opinion . . . for once resulted in no serious dispute between regular critics and the Pulitzer volunteers."[1]

All of these plays deal with timely topics. *This Is New York* is concerned with the New York of the Prohibition era and superimposes upon this background two pompous spokesmen for bourgeois Midwestern morality in the persons of Senator Krull and his wife. *The Petrified Forest* is more a Depression type of play in which the themes of homelessness and personal isolation come to the fore as they do later in such plays as Odets's *Night Music* or Steinbeck's *Of Mice and Men,* or in a novel such as *The Grapes of Wrath. Idiot's Delight* concentrates on a highly strained international situation and speculates upon a war which has not yet erupted but which is to begin within three years of the writing of the play.

It is interesting to note that the concern in these three plays broadened significantly from concern with a domestic issue to concern with a domestic issue which had broader social and cultural implications than did Prohibition, and ultimately to an international issue, the dimensions of which were sufficient to eclipse the issues of the two previous plays. Part of Sherwood's popularity lay in his timeliness, and the three plays to be discussed indicate clearly just how timely he was in his choice of topics.

I   This Is New York

This Is New York is in large part a defense of the nation's most populous city and of the people who inhabit it. In his introduction to the play, Robert Sherwood notes: "So divinely equable is the system of representation in our republic that it has taken approximately twelve qualified citizens on Manhattan Island to equal the voting power of one rural Iowan"* (Preface, xiv-xv). Having thus taken his stand and prepared at least his reading audience, he then introduces the Honorable Harvey L. Krull, United States Senator from South Dakota, and his domineering, pig-headed, self-righteous, crusading wife, Mrs. Krull. The only favorable thing that one can say about the Krulls is that they have spawned a daughter who is realistic enough to take a stand against her parents while obviously retaining her filial devotion to them and who is witty enough to be able to joke about being named Emma Krull. *This Is New York* is really Emma Krull's play, and in it she comes to represent the happy synthesis of the stability of the Midwest and the sophistication of New York.

The first acts of most of Robert Sherwood's plays are somewhat relaxed. Unfortunately, the first act of *This Is New York* comes at times to a virtual standstill. The reinforcement of the attitudes ascribed to the Krulls—and by extension to Midwesterners—becomes repetitive before the scene is out. The tension which is built up first by the turn which Hauser's interview takes when he begins to ask Senator Krull about Emma's rumored engagement to Joseph Gresham, Jr., and later when Gresham appears on the scene, is dissipated by carrying the action on for too long. Some cutting would have resulted in a stronger first act, and this could easily have been achieved by omitting the portions of the act in which the waiters bring food to the Krulls' suite and by shortening the interview between Joe and Emma.

Senator Krull is a stereotyped character. He is a typical isolationist; he is not overly bright; he is much concerned with the opinions of the home folk upon whose votes he is so completely dependent. His concern about his daughter is based upon his fear that she might do something which would lose him votes. Sherwood might have had Krull react with less self-concern to the crisis in which he finds his daughter in the third

*All references are to the first edition of the play (New York: Charles Scribner's Sons, 1931).

act; however, the senator remains the pompous politician throughout the play and never achieves any stature beyond that of a political automaton. This characterization is clearly what Sherwood intends, and it is not defective. It is used effectively, indeed, to give emphasis to one of the play's basic tenets—the corrupted New Yorkers, living lasciviously and wallowing in sins ranging from bootlegging to lesbianism, have far more humanity than the righteous senator and his incredibly "good" wife who is ". . . a power of no mean proportions in the D. A. R., the W. C. T. U., the National Federation of Women's Clubs, and Washington Society," and who ". . . delivers almost every speech with the positive assurance of a 9.2.-inch howitzer" (8). Obviously, Sioux Falls' first citizens do not begin to have the depth of feeling nor the capacity for love that a character such as Harry Glassman, the bootlegger, has. Further, it is clear that the Krulls would make political capital of the institution of marriage were their daughter docile enough to permit them to do so.

One must notice in *This Is New York* that the Krulls represent, for the most part, a negative and restrictive outlook toward society, but those who pass through Phyllis Adrian's apartment, even though they are not respectable by bourgeois standards, are largely positive in their approaches and outlooks.

Emma Krull is not unlike the leading ladies in other Sherwood plays. She is self-possessed and shrewd. She is a realist and is completely competent to control her own destiny. She has her mother's drive and her mother's ability to meet and bring order to difficult situations. Yet there is every hope that she will not turn into the sort of woman her mother has become. It is apparent in Emma's dealings with Phyllis Adrian that Mrs. Krull's shortcomings will not be perpetuated in her daughter. Surely there is none of Mrs. Krull's pompousness in a girl who can say, "I swear I don't know what it is that makes him [Joe Gresham] want to marry me. It must be that he wants my body" (36). This line, of course, is a typical Sherwood line, comparable to a line which he gives to Amytis: "I was just wondering what it would be like to be despoiled."[2]

The credibility of Emma's reaction to her fiancé's mistress has been questioned.[3] Certainly it can be said that the two women react very well to each other. However, this reaction is well prepared for. Emma knows of Joe's various indiscretions and is fully aware of what his relationship to Phyllis Adrian has been. She desires nothing more than to have the way cleared for her marriage to Joe. She stands in awe of Miss Adrian before she ever meets her, as is made clear by her line, "Phyllis Adrian . . . Oh, if I only had a name like that!" (60). Actually Phyllis Adrian represents a glamor which Emma would very much like to possess. It is as much a desire to meet this glamorous creature as it is to try to bring about a settlement between Joe and her that motivates Emma to go to Phyllis's apartment in the first place.

As Phyllis is presented, it would be difficult for one to feel anger toward her. She might well be exasperating; but she is obviously a business woman who is protecting her own interests, and one can scarcely loathe her for this. She is completely frank and honest in what she is doing; she is living very strictly within standards, albeit these are individual ones. *She* is a person; but Mrs. Krull, living her life in such a way as to attempt to meet the standards of the D. A. R., the W. C. T. U., and other such groups, is a social pastiche, a blank woman. She, despite her loud voice and positive opinions, is a face in the crowd and realizes it. She would counter her subconscious dissatisfaction with this situation by forcing everyone else into the crowd.

Since *This Is New York* admittedly represents the conflict between metropolitan America and non-metropolitan America and since the play leaves one thinking that humanity is where one finds it, Sherwood might have made his point more successfully had he done more to illuminate the backgrounds of such people as Phyllis Adrian and Harry Glassman. The only such illumination found in this play is in reference to Harry's paramour, Clarisse Peretti, who allegedly comes from Little Rock; however, she never appears on stage and is used merely to bring about a final clash. Nevertheless, a point is made through her and she is a sympathetic character in the play. She is a drug addict and is living with Harry out of wedlock, but she is madly in love with him and has been for a number of years. Even though she has become something of a wild woman because of her craving for drugs, there is something much more touching and much purer about her relationship with Harry than there is in the relationship between Senator Krull and his wife. Clarisse and Harry have not been denatured by their society; they have not become speech-making zeros.

The psychological portrayal of Mrs. Krull is a sound invention. Mrs. Krull, like the vast majority of social paragons, has a rigid personality. She has, one might venture, gone through life beset by an overwhelming fear of her own real desires, and this overwhelming fear has led to an increasing lack of inner security. Her insecurity, in turn, has led to increased rigidity in her personality. When she protests that she will not leave the hotel suite until Joseph Gresham has left, she is transferring her distrust of herself to her daughter. In the third act, when it is revealed to the Krulls that Phyllis has been Joe Gresham's mistress, Mrs. Krull says: "I don't care to stay here Harvey" (159); but, in view of the situation, she has little choice. She tells her husband that he is degrading himself by entering into any discussion with Phyllis Adrian (169), but, through all of this exchange, it is obvious that what is bothering Mrs. Krull more than anything else is that she has an underlying fascination for what is going on, and that this fascination frightens and threatens her.

From this interpretation of Mrs. Krull's personality, one can generalize further and indicate that the conflict which Sherwood sees existing between New York and the rest of the country is based upon fear and envy, and that the fear and envy are based upon the fact that the rest of the country has only a superficial knowledge of the *real* New York, just as Mrs. Krull has only a superficial knowledge of the people with whom she is suddenly thrust into contact. Just as Emma has the perspicacity to know that there is a real Phyllis Adrian beneath the façade, so has she the insight which permits her to take New York in her stride. She does not turn her back on her heritage; rather, she persists in loving her heritage, as she persists in loving her parents, but she continues to grow and broaden the scope of her appreciations. Emma and her mother are *essentially* the same person; the only variation is that Emma always tries to see the mean, while her mother always sees the extremes and, being threatened by one extreme, retreats to the other.

The structure of *This Is New York* represents a technical achievement for Sherwood. The play conforms quite closely to the standard pattern of progression. The decision is obvious early in Emma's interview with Joe Gresham in the first act. The grappling with difficulties is manifold, and the difficulties are all related to each other: Emma's parents object to the union; Joe is being blackmailed by his former mistress; and at one point Joe decides that he cannot marry Emma. The test of strength is twofold, for both the expected clash, the objection of Emma's parents to the marriage, and the final clash, the tension brought about by Clarisse's suicide, involve tests of strength; and, in each of these tests, Emma proves her strength incontrovertibly. There is, perhaps, a slight irony in the fact that Joe does not prove his strength. Sherwood might have produced a more hopeful play had Joe shown more dynamism in his personal development as the action progressed.[4]

There was less out-and-out negative criticism of *This Is New York* than might have been expected of a play which did not meet the high standard of an earlier play by the same author. *The Road to Rome* still cast its long shadow on Sherwood. Francis Ferguson felt that the tempo of the show was monotonous and that there was need for a heightening of the burlesque elements and for better timing; however, he said that the play was written ". . . with some gusto," and that it ". . . escapes the melancholy fate of *Grand Hotel* by way of the happy American wisecrack and the sweet native wedding-bells finale."[5] While this is a rather backhanded compliment, it certainly is not the sort of criticism which would keep people from going to see the play.

There was some negative criticism about the Broadway presentation of the play. Otis Chatfield-Taylor considered there to be an ". . . almost complete detachment between the script and the way it is played."[6] He felt that there were many wise and witty lines and that the second-act climax was well achieved; but, aside from that, he was unenthusiastic about the production.

In terms of Sherwood's total production, *This Is New York* is a deficient, disappointing piece. However, it is historically significant in that it represents the author's first attempt to create the sort of microcosm which he used with such notable success in *The Petrified Forest* and in *Idiot's Delight*. *This Is New York* is a hesitant step along an uncertain path; but this path was to lead Sherwood to a much broader and much straighter road which was to have its termination in a Pulitzer Prize play within six years.

II   The Petrified Forest

The Petrified Forest is the most consciously allegorical of Robert Sherwood's dramas. Written in a mere four weeks while the author was in Reno obtaining his divorce from Mary Brandon, the play is a social and philosophical commentary with a bittersweet ending.

The Black Mesa Filling Station and Bar-B-Q is in eastern Arizona close to the New Mexico line. Not far from the filling station is the Petrified Forest, a vestigial remainder of prehistory, captured in stone and gawked at by the curious who cannot begin to conceive the immensity of time to which the forest, by its very existence, attests. The mention of the forest early in the play serves to set the philosophical tone for what is to follow. With allusions to the timeless forest constantly in the background, ephemeral men play out their small dramas in the tawdry surroundings of the greasy cafe and drab filling station which Sherwood creates. The filling station ". . . is a place out of space and time where certain men can meet and realize that they are not only individuals but phenomena as well."[7]

The first act moves along at an unhurried pace and is used to introduce most of the characters who are involved in the tense drama of the second act. The play opens in the lunch room of the Bar-B-Q. Two telegraph linemen are having a meal and are talking. The linemen have no organic relation to the play's development except insofar as they introduce through their conversation the important theme of the play that the pioneer is passing away. The remaining pioneer at Black Mesa is Gramp Maple who becomes incensed at the first lineman because of his speech: "Why do you suppose it is that Russia's got the whole world scared? It's because they're pushing ahead. They're pioneering!"* (10). Gramp launches into a diatribe upon the pioneering which he has done, but his words ring false. It is quite clear that the American pioneer is just as much a fossilized remain as the Petrified Forest.

*All references are to the first edition of the play (New York: Charles Scribner's Sons, 1935).

Involved in the running of the Bar-B-Q and filling station are Boze Hertzlinger, a boy in his late teens or early twenties; Gramp's son, Jason Maple, a forty-year-old veteran of World War I who is described as ". . . dull, defeated . . . solemn, bespectacled, paunchy" (8); and Jason's daughter, Gabby, who is ". . . young and pretty, with a certain amount of style about her [and with] . . . an odd look of resentment in her large, dark eyes" (13). Gabby's mother is a French woman who married Jason when he served in France with the army and who came back to Black Mesa with him, only to flee after a short time because she could not stand the isolation of eastern Arizona. She has returned to France and remarried. Gabby has no first-hand memory of her mother, but she has a romantic impression of her and a deep sentiment for her. Her dream is to go to France one day. Meanwhile, she reads François Villon and speaks with the colorful vocabulary of a cowhand. Boze thinks he is in love with Gabby; but obviously he has no understanding of her. The subtleties of her personality escape him utterly, and his concern with her is primarily a physical one.

Gabby is at once the dreamer and the realist. Her heart is in France and her mind is often on the lines of Villon. However, she is another of Sherwood's realistic women, who faces the situation she is in and adjusts to it as well as she can. She does not sentimentalize, nor does she romanticize her situation. The face which she presents to the world is one in which her speech is peppered with "goddams" and her defenses are up against anyone who might try to find any faint glimmering of femininity beneath the carapace which she has constructed and pulled herself into. No one has succeeded in striking a responsive chord in Gabby until Alan Squier appears in the Bar-B-Q. Squier, a destitute writer, has recently arrived from France and has hitch-hiked across the country as far as Black Mesa. During his dinner, which, being bankrupt, he is unable to pay for, he talks with Gabby and it becomes clear almost at once that the two are of the same fiber—that there is spiritual kinship between them. Gabby trusts Squier to the point that she discusses Villon with him and finally shows him the watercolors which she works on surreptitiously and which she has never shown to anyone save Paula, the Mexican cook.

Squier is portrayed as being representative of the positive

forces of civilization. He is intelligent and gifted; he is sophisticated and cultivated. But there is no place for him in this society. He is bankrupt, completely at the end of his possibilities. Sherwood would have us believe that Squier is a valuable but obsolete member of society, and that society is the poorer because he is obsolete. His life crosses Gabby's for thirty minutes, she stakes him to his meal, gives him a silver dollar, and arranges with another customer at the Bar-B-Q, an Ohio banker who is traveling west with his wife and chauffeur, for him to get a lift into Phoenix. He walks out of the Bar-B-Q and, for all intents and purposes, out of Gabby's life forever.

However, word has been received that Duke Mantee, a desperado, has fled from Oklahoma City after taking part in a prison break and massacre there and that he is headed for the Mexican border which would take him through the Black Mesa region. Jason Maple has already gone out with his American Legion cronies to try to apprehend Mantee; therefore Gabby, Gramp, and Boze are left alone in the cafe after Squier and the Chisholms leave for Phoenix. It is only a matter of minutes before Mantee and three of his henchmen arrive and take over the Bar-B-Q. During the last minutes of the first act, Duke Mantee chats affably with his captives and is especially taken by Gramp Maples. Gramp, quite in his glory, treats Duke almost condescendingly, telling him tall tales about some of the desperadoes he has known. Shortly before the act closes, Alan Squier returns to the Bar-B-Q; he has come for help because Mantee has stopped the Chisholms and taken their car, leaving his car for them with the keys inside and the doors locked. Squier, of course, becomes one of the captives, but he takes this with good grace and talks pleasantly with Mantee who seems to be relishing this momentary respite in his flight. Only Boze seems not to be enjoying himself. His middle-class sense of right and wrong intrude upon his judgment and he makes such inconsequential adolescent utterances as "He's a gangster and a rat!" (92), largely in preparation for his attempt to play hero in the second act. Both Gramp and Squier can appreciate the primitive sort of anarchy which Mantee stands for. Gramp can say quite genuinely, "Yes, *sir*—it sure is pleasant to have a killer around here again," and Squier can reply, "Yes. It's pleasant to be back again—among the living. . . . Hooray!" (94).

It is, of course, part of Sherwood's intention not only to praise the man of action, even though he be outside the legal boundaries of society, but also to indicate categorically that the man of action is doomed just as the man of ideas, as represented by Squier, is doomed. Sherwood's intention is made quite clear in his introductions of these two characters. Of Squier he says, ". . . There is something about him—and it is impossible in a stage direction to say just what it is—that brings to mind the ugly word 'condemned'" (30). And in his introduction of Duke Mantee he writes, ". . . There is, about him, one quality of resemblance to Alan Squier: he too is unmistakably condemned" (82). It is apparent, too, that another man of action, Gramp has also been condemned and that, as a pioneer, at least, he has been executed by advancing years. The pioneer is dead and only the exaggerated memory of him remains.

The Petrified Forest has the makings of a popular play on a purely literal level, and this level is, indeed, so appealing that many critics have had difficulty seeing very far beyond it. Actually, the philosophical dimension is not firmly affixed to the melodrama until well into the second act. Alan Squier has been drinking steadily, and the liquor makes him both volubly philosophical and brave. He tells Duke: "I'm planning to be buried in the Petrified Forest. I've been evolving a theory about that that would interest you. It's a graveyard of the civilization that's been shot from under us. It's the world of outmoded ideas. Platonism—patriotism—Christianity—Romance—the economics of Adam Smith—they're all so many dead stumps in the desert. That's where I belong—and so do you, Duke. For you're the last great apostle of rugged individualism. Aren't you?" (113-14). This passage is a succinct statement of the problem of the play.

As the scene progresses, Squier comes more and more to think about Gabby's plight in the desert and to feel that she should be able to go to France and fulfill her dreams. He knows that the only obstacle in her way is that Gramp will not sell the Bar-B-Q and filling station so that she will have enough money to go away. He also knows that Gramp has over twenty thousand dollars in a bank in Santa Fe. He mulls all of this over as he sits and drinks, and at last calls Gramp a mean old miser and asks, "Why in God's name don't you die and do the world some good?" (120). This, of course, is the germ from which grows Squier's great idea of *self*-sacrifice. His future is not worth much, but he does have a five thousand dollar insurance policy, the proceeds from which will enable Gabby to buy her future. Squier endorses his policy over to Gabby (126-27), and makes a compact with Duke to be killed. He has already called Mantee ". . . another child of Nature" (118); now he says to him: "You see, Duke—in killing me—you'd only be executing the sentence of the law—I mean, natural law—survival of the fittest . . ." (130-31). Mantee does not take Squier seriously at first, but, finally convinced of his sincerity, he agrees to do the deed in such a way that Gabby will think that a cold-blooded murder has been committed. Duke is to choose his own moment for the killing.

This turn in the play heightens the tension of an already tense situation and brings audience interest and involvement to a peak. Sherwood has prepared for this development very carefully, so that a situation which might easily be unconvincing to an audience is taken quite in stride. Alan is accepted as the impractical dreamer. Further, in the first act he says, "Let there be killing! All evening long, I've had a feeling of Destiny closing in." He continues, ". . . just now, as I was walking along that road, I began to feel the enchantment of this desert. I looked up at the sky and the stars seemed to be reproving me, mocking me. They were pointing the way to that gleaming sign [outside the Bar-B-Q], and saying, 'There's the end of your tether!'" (93). The writing of Squier's part throughout the play reinforces the author's initial description of the hitch-hiking dreamer as "condemned." He is condemned in much the way that the dinosaurs were as the earth's crust hardened. But, rather than live out the transitional period as generations of suffering dinosaurs must have and rather than be what he colorfully calls "Homo Semi-Americans" (65), he choses to make his death have some meaning. He decrees when and how his death will occur and he imbues it with meaning, albeit of a very materialistic kind. But this, too, is meaningful; for, in an age when idealism is being killed, materialism is all that remains.

Squier basically represents a non-productive man with a death wish. He has produced a book, but it has not sold. He has married, but he has not had children. He is now engaged in what he calls "gipsying": "I had a vague idea that I'd like to see the Pacific Ocean and perhaps drown in it" (33). He is engaged in some sort of vaguely defined spiritual quest when he comes into the Black Mesa Bar-B-Q: "I've been looking for something to believe in. I've been hoping to find something that's worth living for—and dying for" (52). Squier is a remnant of the lost generation who quotes passages from *The Hollow Men* and calls their message ". . . discouraging, because it's true" (62). Squier's attack of serious introspection is not unusual in the literature of the 1930's. But it is interesting to follow the outcome in this particular case. Having admittedly been on a quest for something worth living and, indeed, dying for, Squier finally thinks he has found what he has been questing after and willingly makes his sacrifice so that Gabby can leave Black Mesa and go to France. But he has already told her, "I'd stay here, Gabrielle, and avoid disappointment. . . . I've been to France. . . . I lived there for eight years, through seventeen changes of government" (49-50).

In giving up his life for Gabby, Squier claims that "She may be one of the immortal women of France—another Joan of Arc, or Georges Sand, or Madame Curie" (132). This is, of course, romantic tripe. It is followed by an utterance which would be more convincing coming from the love-struck Boze than from the representative of sophisticated intelligence, Squier: "Any woman is worth everything that any man has to give—anguish, ecstasy, faith, jealousy, love, hatred, life or death" (136). And by some strange perversion of logic, he calls this man's excuse for existence. It is obvious that the development of Squier's personality in the play is often faulty and that his decline can not be attributed alone to the quantities of whiskey which he drank during his captivity in the Bar-B-Q.

John Howard Lawson points to a definite weakness in the play when he says that it states a problem but does not ". . . show the working out of the problem as it affects the shifting balance between man and his environment."[8] He goes on to say that Sherwood cannot do this ". . . because he forewarns us that Squier is a man whose conscious will has atrophied."[9] He points out the similarity between Squier and Trophimof in *The Cherry Orchard*, but he states that because of Sherwood's static point of view his is a drama of attrition, whereas Chekhov's drama is a drama of sheer art.

The most significant point that Mr. Lawson makes is that "Sherwood's thought follows the time-worn cycle: the philosophy of blood and nerves leads to pessimism; the denial of reason leads to the acceptance of violence."[10] And it is just this implication that gives frightening overtones to the philosophical cargo which *The Petrified Forest* carries. There is nothing substantial to build on as this play runs its course. If Duke Mantee shows a spark of humanity, certainly the upholders of the "right" who are pursuing him do not. They are anxious only to shoot and kill; they are frighteningly blood-thirsty. When Duke and his accomplices have run from the Bar-B-Q, taking hostages with them, Herb, the Legionnaire, and the Sheriff and his deputies want to begin shooting. Jason reminds them that there are innocent people on the running-board of the fleeing car, and Herb answers: "Never mind 'em! Let's shoot the hell out of 'em!" (171). These pursuers pay no attention to the dying Alan Squier; their concern is with the hunt.

Sherwood's presentation of the Ohio banker, Chisholm, and his wife, has point. Chisholm represents a sort of atrophied wealth. Squier dies to give Gabby what her grandfather could give her without dying or what the Chisholms could give her without missing it. And Mrs. Chisholm realizes almost as much as Squier what is at stake for Gabby, for in her soliloquy (143) she recounts the sad and frustrating facts of her own youth. She tells of her marriage to her pompous husband who sits aghast and listens to her indictment that "He took my soul and had it stenciled on a card, and filed" (143). Then, when Duke Mantee complains that when one lives the life that he does, ". . . you don't get much chance to be crawling into the hay with some dame," Mrs. Chisholm—her blood warmed by the whiskey she has been quaffing—queries, "I wonder if we could find any hay around here?" (146). When she is asked if this is an offer, she replies quite blandly that it is and that ". . . it was made with all sincerity." Mrs. Chisholm's life with her husband has represented what the world looks upon as respectable love. Yet the love in the play which gives some offer of fulfillment is that which is outside the codes of society: Boze is on the brink of seducing Gabby when he is interrupted by the entrance of the Mantee desperadoes on the scene; Gabby falls in love with Squier and suggests that they go off and live together; Mantee risks being captured because he is waiting at Black Mesa for Doris with whom he is in love.

The ending of *The Petrified Forest* is prolonged beyond the point that it ideally should be. After Squier is shot, Gabby steadies him and helps him into a chair. He says to her, "It doesn't hurt—or, at least, it doesn't seem [to]" (171). Actually the play might well have ended at this point. The remainder is so anticlimactic that it is bothersome and disappointing.

The play had a successful run on Broadway and, as has been noted, was made into a film. The critical reception of *The Petrified Forest* was overwhelmingly favorable. Grenville Vernon credited its author with laying ". . . over the rough bones of an impossible story . . . the patina of real brilliancy."[11] Stark Young called "The formula of its comic portions . . . Shavian," and he welcomed the play as ". . . a rest from the bourgeois seriousness of many of our plays."[12]

Without saying anything negative about the play, the critic for *Literary Digest* pointed to one of the play's obvious weaknesses when he called *The Petrified Forest* ". . . a smooth and glossy entertainment."[13] It is the gloss which has caused some later critics to question the artistic caliber of the play. The same critic recognized that "The second [act], suddenly, is exciting, filled with tension, and makes its points with a thump."[14] The tension which is roused in this act arises within the play more than it exists in situations outside the immediate action. Were the play simply about Duke Mantee's taking over of the Black Mesa Bar-B-Q, the tension would not be from within. However, the expected clash, the killing of Alan Squier, adds a new tension to the last third of the play; and this tension is heightened as Alan, happy in his love for Gabby, makes such statements as "It [the sound of the deputies shooting their guns] almost restores in me the will to live—and love—and conquer" (163). And the qualifying word "almost" helps to keep the tension high, for it prevents the statement from representing a change of heart in Alan.

It is, of course, the expected clash which makes the play, as Miss Wyatt called it, "breathless." Whether Miss Wyatt is correct in her enthusiastic statement that Sherwood has ". . . teased a bit of romance out of every spirit and has shot poetry out of the last rattle of the machine gun,"[15] may be seriously questioned. At any rate, the immense success of the play—following quite rapidly on the heels of *Reunion in Vienna* which had scored a distinct triumph on Broadway—did, as a Canadian critic put it, ". . . definitely establish Sherwood's right to be ranked as one of the leading American dramatists."[16] The play represented a fruition of Sherwood's struggle toward finding a form through which to express philosophical ideas. Where he had bungled in *This Is New York,* he came directly to grips with the effective use of his contrived microcosm in *The Petrified Forest.*

III   Idiot's Delight

Maxwell Anderson and Laurence Stallings wrote *What Price Glory?* in 1924 and concluded it with the words, "What a lot of goddam fools it takes to make a war." Twelve years later, when news of the Spanish Civil War and of the Italian invasion of Ethiopia occupied the headlines, and when Hitler was rattling his saber ominously over his neighbors in eastern Europe, Robert Sherwood presented audiences with *Idiot's Delight* which reflected the growing anti-war sentiment in the United States in the mid-1930's. Sherwood's message is somewhat different from that of Anderson and Stallings. In the postscript to his play he writes, ". . . let me express here the conviction that those who shrug and say, 'War is inevitable,' are false prophets. I believe that the world is populated largely by decent people, and decent people don't want war. Nor do they make war. They fight and die, to be sure—but that is because they have been deluded by their exploiters, who are members of the indecent minority"* (189). This sentiment represents a mellowing from the attitude expressed implicitly in *The Petrified Forest* in the characterization of the blood-thirsty Legionnaires, who have "fought to make the world safe for democracy," who love to shoot and kill, and who care little whether they are shooting at the just or the unjust.

It is clear that the sentiment in *Idiot's Delight* is that human conflict is largely the fault of those who make it possible, in this specific case, the munitions manufacturer, Achilles Weber. His

*All references are to the first edition of the play (New York: Charles Scribner's Sons, 1936).

Russian mistress, Irene, realizes this fact; and, when war finally erupts, she cries out to Weber: "All this great, wonderful death and destruction, everywhere. And you promoted it!" But Weber, who whimsically declines to take all the credit, retorts: ". . . But don't forget to do honor to Him—up there—who put fear into man. I am the humble instrument of His divine will" (103). And again Weber declines to accept the full responsibility for his part in bringing about conflict when he asks Irene, ". . . who are the greater criminals—those who sell the instruments of death, or those who buy them, and use them?" (107). The question of responsibility, of course, is the compelling question of the age, and it recurs in such works as Clifford Odets' *Golden Boy,* Arthur Miller's *All My Sons,* Paul Green's *Johnny Johnson,* Maxwell Anderson's *Winterset,* and a host of other plays of the 1930's and '40's. By shifting responsibility, the foul deed can be done, yet everyone involved can be exonerated. The "indecent minority" is a minority of faceless buck-passers.

One of the major points of *Idiot's Delight* had been made ten years earlier in *The Road to Rome,* when Amytis deflated Hannibal after he had stated that he had been motivated in his conquests by the voice of his god, Ba-al, and she had replied: "That wasn't the voice of Ba-al, Hannibal. That was the voice of the shopkeepers of Carthage, who are afraid that Rome will interfere with their trade. . . . Hatred, greed, envy, and the passionate desire for revenge—those are the high ideals that inspire you soldiers, Roman and Carthaginian alike."[17] In *Idiot's Delight,* Ba-al is dead, and the ancient god of the Hebrews has been reduced to a ". . . poor, lonely old soul. Sitting up in heaven, with nothing to do, but play solitaire. Poor, dear God. Playing Idiot's Delight. The game that never means anything, and never ends" (104). This is the God of a skeptical age, and this is life in Spenglerian terms or in terms of the philosophy of T. S. Eliot in *The Waste Land* or in *The Hollow Men,* where life *does* end, but with a whimper rather than a bang.

Harold Clurman has called the sentiment which led Sherwood to write *Idiot's Delight* cogent. He has very astutely and perceptively noted that the play ". . . echoes the American fear of and profound estrangement from the facts of European intrigue which led to war," and he supports this contention by reminding readers that Sherwood's French pacifist, Quillery, is cast as a Radical-Socialist who venerated Lenin; but, in reality, the Radical-Socialists of pre-war France were the small business-men who hated Lenin.[18] But Clurman praises the play for giving "... us an inkling of the moral climate in our country" during this period of crisis. Clurman also makes the point that during this time "... the attitude of our dramatists, generally speaking, was fundamentally moral rather than, as some are now inclined to believe, political."[19]

This, of course, is a disputed point, and Casper H. Nannes presents a case for *Idiot's Delight* as political drama in *Politics in the American Drama*,[20] in which he claims, quite validly, that Sherwood's anti-war bias reached its peak in *Idiot's Delight*" (153). Actually Sherwood's stand in regard to war is much easier to understand and to accept as a moral rather than as a political stand. Surely the attitude which he is working toward in *Abe Lincoln in Illinois* and which he finally achieves in his propagandistic *There Shall Be No Night* is a moral stand. The fact that both of these plays are closer temporally to audiences than was a play such as *The Road to Rome* can easily mislead them into seeing the more immediate political implications of what Sherwood is saying than the moral implications. How-ever, it is clear, especially in the case of *There Shall Be No Night*, that had the play been fundamentally political rather than moral, Sherwood could not in good conscience have rewritten it in 1943 and changed the nationality of the chief contending parties in the action from Finnish to Greek. And those critics who castigated him for "dumping the Finns" were obviously insensi-tive to the underlying purpose of this play, and perhaps of all of his plays which dealt with the problem of war.

Sherwood managed to put more tension into *Idiot's Delight* than he was able to achieve in many of his other plays. The uncertainty that the people assembled in the Italian *pensione* will be permitted to cross the border into Switzerland pervades the play and causes the characters to show tension in their various ways. The tension is enhanced by the sounding of air raid sirens, and it reaches a peak with the execution of Quillery. However, John Mason Brown understates a very important point when he writes that "The tension in Europe added to the tension of *Idiot's Delight*."[21] The play capitalized on this tension increasingly at every performance. It opened in New York two days after Italy had invaded Ethiopia; it opened in London less than a week after Hitler's forces had marched into Austria. It played amid constant international tensions, and even its most successful revival came in 1951 at a time when an undeclared war was being fought at great cost of human life in Korea.

Sherwood had to exercise considerable control to make *Idiot's Delight* as serious a play as he did. More than any other Sherwood drama, this play has a message. It was written with great intensity, indeed with such great intensity that its author wrote on one occasion until well past midnight, went to bed, but couldn't stand not knowing the outcome of the second act; so he arose again at three and continued writing until dawn.[22] The play, which was written and presented to the Lunts in a period of two weeks, was not entirely ready for Broadway in its original form. Sherwood had once said, "The trouble with me is that I start off with a big message and end with nothing but good entertainment,"[23] and *Idiot's Delight* is an especially apt case in point. At one of the early rehearsals, Lawrence Langner pointed out that the play seemed too light for its very serious content. This was a thoughtful observation for at this point, as Langner notes, the play ". . . had drifted perilously between the delightful story of a group of chorus girls lost in Italy, and the more serious implications of the oncoming war."[24]

Lynn Fontanne, as well as Alfred Lunt and Robert Sherwood, agreed with Langner's analysis; and, after considerable pondering, Miss Fontanne suggested that Sherwood write into the play a significant scene for her—she played Irene—and Achilles Weber, the munitions baron. Sherwood did so, and the play took on a more serious tone, even though this increased seriousness was attained through means which did not detract from the play's initial humor and pleasing pace. Also, the irony of the play was increased by this change; and, through the increased irony, Weber's personality was projected more fully to the audience. His unchivalrous abandonment of Irene, an abandonment to almost certain death, is directly attributable to the fact that Irene expresses pacifist sentiments. The munitions manufacturer will tolerate no threat to his commercial interests in the form of such sentiments; by abandoning Irene, he shows himself unmistakably to be a man with no fundamental loyalties. One might compare Weber to Robert Murray in *Small War on Murray Hill*; Murray shows similar tendencies, although his personality in Sherwood's later play is just sketched in, whereas Achilles Weber is a more fully realized character in *Idiot's Delight*.

The microcosm which Sherwood creates in *Idiot's Delight* is suggestive of a diminutive *Magic Mountain*, translated into American terms. The characterization is of the utmost importance in Sherwood's play, just as it is in Mann's novel, for each character is a broad representative of a specific *Weltanschauung*; each speaks for a large class.

Harry Van is the prototypical "hoofer" and is virtually a master of ceremonies in the play. He represents American views much more fully than does the other male American in the play, Don Navadel. Van has a marked feeling of loyalty to his girls, but he also has a feeling of loyalty to Irene, the phony Russian countess, because he is convinced that he spent the night with her once in Kansas City, but even more so because she apparently remembers that they spent the night together and has some sentiment about it. Harry is the peacemaker, but this writer feels—with Grenville Vernon who reviewed the play for *Commonweal*[25]—that Harry is artistically false. His chief function in much of the play is that of pace-setter. Harry denounces war, but he never really presents any significant arguments for doing so. He is statically pacifistic in his presentation. Further, his heroic action in coming back to the *pensione* to die with Irene is not convincing. He has not, like Alan Squier, shown a death wish. His death does not lead to anything greater. He is representative of meaningless action, as is the French pacifist, Quillery.

Harry Van's philosophy is never really expressed clearly. The closest he comes to expressing any sort of idealogical stand is in the first act when he says to Dr. Waldersee, "All my life . . . I've been selling phoney goods to people of meagre intelligence and great faith. You'd think that would make me contemptuous of the human race, wouldn't you? But—on the contrary—it has given *me* faith. It has made me sure that no matter how much the meek may be bulldozed or gypped they *will* eventually inherit the earth" (61). The thinking in this passage is so confused and inconsistent that one can scarcely generalize about

Harry's philosophy from it; yet this is typical of Harry's more serious utterances.

Quillery is often somewhat less than convincing in much the same way that Harry Van is. Having attempted to be a citizen of the world, Quillery very suddenly becomes a Frenchman again when war is declared. He is opinionated and dogmatic, but very insecure psychologically. He has fuzzy notions of how to bring about a better world, and he becomes an immature social boor when he begins to expand his hazy theories. He feels that the strongest force in the world is ". . . the mature intelligence of the workers of the world! There is one antidote for war —Revolution!" (41).

Quillery is used to point the finger unquestionably at Achilles Weber. Having reached a frenzied state of anti-war sentiment, he tells Cherry, the Englishman, that Weber ". . . can give you all the war news. Because he *made* it. . . . He has been organizing the arms industry. Munitions. To kill French babies. And English babies" (79). In the following scene, Irene is to become even more graphic in describing the horror of what Weber is making possible when she speaks of what the war will be like: A young woman ". . . lying in a cellar that has been wrecked by an air raid, and her firm young breasts are all mixed up with the bowels of a dismembered policeman, and the embryo from her womb is splattered against the face of a dead bishop" (105). As Irene's pacifism grows, it seems that she would be more appealing to Quillery than to Harry Van; and Sherwood might indeed have added credibility to the play had he spared Quillery rather than having him executed by the Fascisti. Had Quillery returned to the *pensione* to remain with Irene, the action would have been as convincing as was Boze's action in *The Petrified Forest* when he risked his life and grabbed Mantee's gun.

In many respects Quillery is suggestive of Boze. He is utterly lacking in objectivity and is very egocentric. He is a master of the hollow insult, as Boze was. His speech to Dr. Waldersee exemplifies this quality: "The eminent Dr. Hugo Waldersee. A wearer of the sacred swastika. Down with the Communists! Off with their heads! So that the world may be safe for the Nazi murderers" (80). He then turns on the British couple, the Cherrys, and insults them by saying, "And now we hear the voice of England! The great, well-fed, pious hypocrite! The grabber—the exploiter—the immaculate butcher! It was *you* forced this war, because miserable little Italy dared to drag its black shirt across your trail of Empire" (81-82).

Despite this tirade, Quillery tells the Italian officers later in the same scene that "England and France are fighting for the hopes of mankind" (115). He then launches into the fanatical diatribe which costs him his life. He shouts, "Down with Fascism! Abbasso Fascismo!" (116). He is placed under arrest by the Italians, who have very little choice but to do this, and he shouts, "Call out the firing squad! Shoot me dead! But do not think you can silence the truth that's in me" (116). These are brave, stirring words; but they are those of a person who has regressed to adolescence and whose idealism leads to nothing but death without meaning. The role is well depicted and, in itself, is credible. However, the play as a whole would have gained in credibility had Quillery been permitted to live and to fall in love with Irene. The reunion of the pathological patriot with the pathological liar would have been much more satisfying than was the reunion of the good-natured Harry Van with Irene.

The Cherrys are brought into the play for two reasons. In the first place, they represent the effect of war upon young love—always an appealing theme. But in a broader sense, they represent the English stand in regard to war. They are restrained and calm. They do not like what is going on, but they do not explode into action as might the more volatile French, represented by Quillery. In this regard, Harry Van represents his country, the United States. He shepherds his girls to the frontier, but he returns for personal reasons to stay with Irene. His involvement in the war is unofficial, but morality leads him to take a stand, even though the bases of this morality are personal and private.

Dr. Waldersee, of course, represents the dilemma of the scientist who is essentially dedicated to something far larger than nationalism, but whose blood tie with his country is great enough to divert him from his scientific pursuits for the benefit of mankind to scientific pursuits which will be quite the opposite. In reality, Dr. Waldersee is faced with the same sort of moral dilemma which faced Dr. Valkonen in *There Shall Be No Night*, and the solution of the conflict, on a moral level at least, is similar in both cases.

Idiot's Delight amazed audiences because Sherwood not only had foreseen the broad outlines of history, but also had dealt with specifics which were in time to be borne out by developments in international politics. The play continued to have a very definite appeal through the early years of the war; and, when it was revived in 1951, audiences were again to be much in awe of Sherwood's ability to prognosticate with such accuracy.

The areas in which *Idiot's Delight* appealed to audiences are as diverse as the areas in which *The Road to Rome* made its appeal. Grenville Vernon, writing a second review of the play six weeks after he had first reviewed it, felt that it ". . . is not all of one piece. It is perhaps even too shrewdly made for popular appeal. It is in its entirety neither comedy, melodrama, musical comedy nor propaganda play. It is by turns all of these . . . there are those who would have wished [Sherwood] had stuck a little closer to artistic unity."[26]

The play's most severe structural flaw is obviously the ending. Bombs are falling, Harry and Irene are in the *pensione,* certainly doomed. Harry has been playing "The Ride of the Walküries." Irene asks him if he knows any hymns, and in jazz time he begins to play "Onward, Christian Soldiers." The irony of this is almost too heavy handed; and, for every critic who agreed with *Newsweek's* critic in calling the ending "a stirring bit of theatre,"[27] there were dozens who felt, like Grenville Vernon, that it was "hokum of a peculiarly annoying kind."[28] Sherwood's intention to represent in *Idiot's Delight* ". . . a compound of bland pessimism and desperate optimism, of chaos and jazz,"[29] is achieved in his ending; but the method to achieve it is so jarringly melodramatic that the impact is all but lost.

In *Idiot's Delight,* Sherwood's out-and-out pacifism is replaced by pessimism. Joseph Wood Krutch has noted that the author's main contention in this play is that ". . . men are too emotional and too childish to carry to a successful issue any plan for abolishing war."[30] This is the first step away from the pacifism of Sherwood's earlier works. In *Idiot's Delight,* the author has not turned his back on pacifism, but he is not hopeful that men will be pacific. The thinking in this play leads directly into *Abe Lincoln in Illinois* and reaches its final culmination in *There Shall Be No Night* with its "Yes, but . . ." attitude.

CHAPTER 4

Of Men and Their Wars

> "We have within ourselves the power to con-
> quer bestiality . . . with the power of the
> light that is in our minds!"
> — *There Shall Be No Night*

FOUR OF SHERWOOD'S PLAYS—*Waterloo Bridge, Abe Lincoln in Illinois, There Shall Be No Night,* and *The Rugged Path,* as well as his only novel, *The Virtuous Knight*—are concerned primarily with the reaction of the protagonist to war. Roy Cronin, the protagonist of *Waterloo Bridge,* is a war-weary soldier who, after three years of service, falls in love and comes perilously close to desertion. Abe Lincoln is pictured as a warm human being, essentially calm and peace-loving, who has to make the tortuous decision that will plunge his nation into a civil war which will seriously threaten the existence of a United States of America. Kaarlo Valkonen is a winner of the Nobel Peace Prize, who has to decide whether to remain in his native Finland when she is being invaded or to flee to a friendly country. Morey Vinion in *The Rugged Path* must decide between fighting the war from behind a desk or in the field; and Martin, Earl of Elcester, drawn into going off to fight in the Crusades, is led in the novel to question the validity of the fight which is being waged, especially when he comes to see it from the perspective of the enemy.

The works treated in this chapter vary greatly in quality. *Waterloo Bridge* is trivial when viewed separately, but is revealing in terms of Sherwood's development as a playwright. *Abe Lincoln in Illinois* is more than just another tribute to the sixteenth President: It is a midpoint between Sherwood's total pacifism as seen in *The Road to Rome* and *Waterloo Bridge* and his philosophy of justified, necessitous resistance, of which *There Shall Be No Night* is representative. *The Rugged Path* is of more philosophical than dramatic interest; it carries the philosophy of *There Shall Be No Night* one step farther and it is revealing in the light of Sherwood's own involvement in World War II. *The Virtuous Knight* is a seriously defective novel; its structure is chaotic, but the whole concept of human conflict is considered quite fully in the book. Sherwood's philosophy regarding war is probably more fully enunciated in this work than in any other.

These five works are very much concerned with the individual and his relation to society. Each of them contains a fully realized portrait of one individual, and through them one can easily see the course which Sherwood's thinking followed from the late 1920's up until the mid-1940's. The kaleidoscopic view which is presented through these plays brings into focus the years of struggle which a sensitive, pacifist artist passed through as he saw his society move from the recovery following one cataclysmic conflict to its involvement in and ultimate emergence from yet another one. *Idiot's Delight,* as has been mentioned in the chapter immediately preceding this one, marked the turning point in Sherwood's thought. His first Pulitzer Prize play represented the nadir of the author's hopes, the low point in his pessimism. From 1936 until the end of World War II, this pessimism persisted in varying degrees and from it emerged a philosophical point of view which had to admit the necessity of defensive struggle in the face of advancing totalitarianism.

Three of Sherwood's four Pulitzer Prizes were awarded to him for plays which were directly concerned with some phase of war: *Idiot's Delight* (1936); *Abe Lincoln in Illinois* (1939); and *There Shall Be No Night* (1941). These plays progressively came to state a theory of political action and involvement. Sherwood's thoughts regarding political action were mirrored in the bulk of the American populace during this period; for, with the advance of Fascism in Europe, it became increasingly evident that passive resistance could result only in subjugation. If audiences in 1936 could nod their heads in agreement as Irene said, "I'll tell you what else you can do in these tragic circumstances. You can refuse to fight!" (*Idiot's Delight,* 176). Most playgoers after 1939 would be more inclined to agree with

Dr. Valkonen's feeling that to fight the Fascists is ". . . To help speed the day when man becomes genuinely human" (*There Shall Be No Night*, 154).

Sherwood, a moral rather than a political pacifist, never ceased to believe that pacifism was the ideal course. He would never have advocated offensive action, and in this respect he remained the pacifist. However, he realized the futility of trying to maintain liberty and of trying to remain totally pacifist in a world which was faced with the problems which Fascist aggression posed in the late 1930's. Those who called him a warmonger after they had seen *There Shall Be No Night* failed to understand what he was advocating. It is to Sherwood's great and enduring credit that he did not bury his head in the sands of pacifism when the entire human race was threatened by forces which would enslave free men.

I   Waterloo Bridge

The plot of *Waterloo Bridge* is as old as literature itself. An unregenerate streetwalker meets an innocent youth who falls in love with her, and she is purified through his love. In this particular case, the purification takes place over the feeble protestations of Myra, the streetwalker in question. Much of the play is melodramatic, and all of it is as sentimental as the author warns in his preface it is going to be. The play can in no sense establish a claim to literary distinction; it is of interest largely because it marks a step in the author's development.

The most serious weakness of *Waterloo Bridge* is the plot. The writing is generally polished and the characterization is handled expertly. But Joseph Wood Krutch's complaints about the play sum up very succinctly what its basic drawbacks are. He claims that in *Waterloo Bridge*, Sherwood ". . . has written, with singularly few variations, the sophomore's story of the Fallen Woman and the Nice Young Man." He continues to say that "Some plays are unconvincing because they are obviously untrue to life; others for no other reason than that they have been seen so often that they inevitably remind one of the theatre; and the present piece belongs to the latter class."[1] Thus, handicapped by the banality of the plot, Sherwood proceeded unhesitatingly to display all of the stock elements which the situation suggested; and the result is that the positive features of his work were obscured almost totally by its negative features.

In defense of the play, it must certainly be admitted that the first scene has a pace unusual for the first act of a Sherwood play. The writing here, while not the work of a consummate artist, is surely the work of a practiced, skillful craftsman. The scene moves rapidly, partly because there are only two characters who have to be developed in it to any extent—Myra and Roy. Kitty is a stock character, as is the military policeman who talks with her. The locale is also somewhat stock—London in an evening during wartime.

Myra Deauville has just returned from somewhere in the depths of Sussex where she has been doing her bit for the war effort, rather incongruously, as a farmerette. She meets her friend Kitty on Waterloo Bridge where Kitty is soliciting with rather meager success because of the impending air raid. They sketch in some necessary background material for the audience as they recount to each other what they have been doing since they last saw each other. The humor is rather broad, and is heavily dependent upon Kitty's cockney accent and urban prejudices. It is revealed shortly that Myra is an American and that she has been in England since before the war because the show in which she was a chorus girl, *The Pink Lady*, closed, leaving her in London without enough money to buy a ticket home. From that time she has been living a hand-to-mouth existence, managing to survive primarily on funds obtained through prostitution. She would like to return home, but she has little hope of being able to do so. Indeed, at the time the play opens, she is not even sure that she will have a roof over her head for that night, because she owes rent to her landlady, Mrs. Hobley, who is holding her trunk and other goods as security.

The play's action takes place in November, 1917, and the winter ahead is not pleasant to think about. Myra tells Kitty, "I noticed the people in the station, and in the streets coming over. They looked as if they was all hurrying to a funeral or something," and Kitty responds that ". . . London's dead. . . . It's going to be a wretched winter"* (19). Kitty has

* All references are to the first edition of the play (New York: Charles Scribner's Sons, 1930).

already noticed a distinct falling off in her business, for military men are getting fewer leaves and the competition for those few who are around is very great. She comments on her own poverty and regrets her inability to help the penniless Myra. She suggests, "What you ought to do is come with me along the Strand and make some money so you can surprise Mrs. 'Obley with the rent" (22), but Myra expresses her doubt that there is much money on the streets tonight. She decides, however, to try to find something, because "If I wait till to-morrow, it'll only be that much harder" (27). This bit of social commentary—the reluctance of the prostitute to ply her trade—is completely typical of plays of this sort and is conventionally used to prepare the way for the change of heart which has to come in the last act.

Myra's Lothario comes stumbling onto the scene in the person of Roy Cronin from Locke's Falls, New York. Roy, like Sherwood, enlisted in a Canadian regiment and he has now been in service for three years. The audience knows that he ". . . wasn't born the day before yesterday" (57), only because Roy tells them so. Actually, he represents all of the gaucherie of the prototypical young soldier abroad. He is remarkably bumptious and innocent; he sees in Myra a paragon of purity; and he promptly falls in love with her, primarily because he is lonely and she is a friendly American. The motive for this romance is psychologically convincing, but is, alas, so hackneyed as to be extremely tiresome.

Roy brings out the best in Myra, or so the audience is to believe. Her original intention is to fleece the young soldier, but she develops an affection for him and cannot take advantage of his innocence. She has to get him out of her life, however, for his presence makes it impossible for her to follow her usual profession. When her attempts to dismiss him fail utterly, she finally consents to make him happy by taking a monthly allowance from him and by letting him name her as beneficiary on his army insurance policy. Myra and Roy have a parting scene on Waterloo Bridge where they first met, then he goes off to war and she, spiritually and materially the richer, is left with the memory of him.

Actually, every turn in *Waterloo Bridge* is so predictable that in seeing it for the first time, one has the peculiar sensation of having seen it many times before. The play might have gained in stature had Sherwood done more to develop the theme of homelessness which pervades the play, presenting his material somewhat as Odets did in *Night Music*; however, as the piece stands, none of its themes is fully realized and the overall effect of the play is garbled.

One significant point which does come through is the impersonality of modern warfare. Roy has always wanted to see a raid on London. When he hears enemy planes overhead, he is exhilarated even though his life is in jeopardy. He says of the pilot, "Just think of the old guy up there with eight million people to aim at" (37). His attitude is completely fatalistic, largely because ". . . the chances are a million to one against a bomb dropping around here" (37). He is playing the odds, and he is playing to win.

Waterloo Bridge seeks to emphasize the fact that modern war is such that one cannot escape from it. When Roy says, "I thought I was on leave away from the war," Myra answers, "You can't get away from this war, soldier" (38). This statement at the end of the first scene has been well illustrated throughout the scene, and it would have given greater thematic substance to the play had it been developed more fully and consistently throughout the remaining scenes.

Roy has, presumably, been a dutiful soldier for three years. He has fought with valor and has been wounded. He has spent months in a hospital being patched up; and, when the action of the play takes place, he is on leave from the hospital. He has grown disenchanted with war, but has not had any positive grounds for questioning what he is doing until his meeting with Myra. Love offers him his first real chance for human fulfillment, and he finds himself ready to desert in order to remain with the one he loves. In one of the play's more impassioned speeches, he says, "For three years I've done everything they told me. I've sloped arms when they told me and saluted when they told me; I've stood up straight when they told me and ducked when they told me. For three years I've played their game. Now, by God, I'm going to play my own" (165-66). These lines might have been written about Oliver Wendell Holmes who reached the same decision that Roy did after he had fought for three years in the Union Army during the Civil War. But Holmes apparently did not have a Myra to convince him that he had to go on fighting, and he actually left his regiment.

When Sherwood writes Roy's last impassioned speech, he is actually delivering his own pacifist diatribe and his vigor is suggestive of that seen in some of the proletarian playwrights of the 1930's. Roy says, "Yes—fight the war! What's the war, anyway? It's that guy up there in his aeroplane. What do I care about him and his bombs? . . . What do I care who he is, or what he does, or what happens to him? That war's over for me. What I've got to fight is the whole dirty world. That's the enemy that's against you and me. That's what makes the rotten mess we've got to live in" (168). This speech might indeed have come directly from the Laboratory Assistant Scene in Odets' *Waiting for Lefty* or it might have been spoken by Steve Takis in *Night Music*.

But, for all his soliloquizing, Roy goes back to war, probably to die for he now sees the utter fraudulency of what he is doing and this will reduce his efficiency as a soldier. Myra, left alone on Waterloo Bridge, flagrantly lights a cigarette and makes herself a target for the airplanes which are heard overhead. And so the play ends, its problems hanging unresolved, on a gloomy note of pessimism. The pessimism is especially great in view of Kitty's speech in which she says, "After the war! And when will that be? To-morrow? No! Next year? No! A 'undred years from now? I doubt it" (131). The implication is that there will be no respite—that the war to end all wars will never really end. In germ, at least, this is the beginning of the pessimism which pervades *Idiot's Delight*.

In a play dealing with the stock situation that *Waterloo Bridge* does, the humanity of the prostitute must apparently emerge as part of the message. Sherwood delivers this message largely through his portrayal of Myra; however, Kitty's participation in the first scene of act two is also vital in this regard. Kitty, more hardened than Myra, provides an excellent contrast. She is basically anti-masculine. No man can move her to sentiment. She works on Roy in Myra's behalf and is quite appalled when Myra will not take what she can get from the young soldier. Kitty's warmth and humanity are illustrated in her protective attitude toward Myra, but Myra's warmth and humanity are illustrated in her ultimate sincerity and honesty in dealing with Roy.

Sherwood is at his best in his presentation of self-righteous elderly women. To a gallery which includes Fabia, Mrs. Chisholm, and Mrs. Krull, one must surely add Mrs. Hobley. Her psychological portrayal is probably the best in the play, even though she is a minor character. Mrs. Hobley is pinched by poverty, but she feels a strong sense of guilt at making a large proportion of her living from renting rooms to young women who are obviously prostitutes. Yet these young women are the only ones who will pay her the amount of rent which she charges for her rather forbidding apartments. Mrs. Hobley victimizes and browbeats her tenants as a means toward assuaging her own guilt feelings.

The real source of Mrs. Hobley's guilt feelings is also interesting to speculate upon although it presumably stems from the causes stated. However, the question of why Mrs. Hobley rents her rooms to prostitutes arises. One would think she might, in crowded, wartime London, garner more respectable tenants were she really troubled by renting to such as Myra. Actually, Mrs. Hobley is seeking an obvious source of guilt to obscure the real source. She is pathologically avaricious, and her avarice leads her into acts of dishonesty as is shown in her dealings with Roy when he wishes to pay her the back rent which Myra owes. Sherwood has presented a carefully conceived characterization in Mrs. Hobley. She is partly a stock character, a troublesome landlady, partly a developing character, a woman obsessed by her own guilt; and Sherwood handles her development with finesse and verisimilitude.

As a pacifist document, *Waterloo Bridge* is too highly personalized and too subjective to have much weight. Stark Young was correct when he assumed that the play was written in haste, and his indictment that ". . . the lines contain no meat of any kind and no dramatic diction, no dialogue with point, no speech that has any reality of any kind or any sort of edge,"[2] is really not unfair. His classification of the play as ". . . rubbish, but well-scrutinized rubbish" is shrewd.

Despite the play's limitations, it had some appeal to audiences and its Broadway run can scarcely be called a failure, although it was a disappointment. As a film produced in 1940, *Waterloo Bridge* was notably successful, depending for its appeal largely

[82]

upon the international situation. The play must be recognized, however, as being weakened by ideological confusion. One recent critic has pinpointed the play's major problem in noting that the ". . . anti-war thought is . . . a thematic anomaly unrelated to the sociological theme which is developed by the play's dramatic structure."[3]

II   Abe Lincoln in Illinois

If Robert Sherwood were to be remembered for any one of his plays, it is likely that the play which would fix his name in the galaxy of the immortals is *Abe Lincoln in Illinois*. The Lincoln play is not his best drama, but more people have probably seen it and been affected by it than by any of his other productions. It has been performed literally thousands of times throughout the United States in large cities and small towns by polished actors and by high school amateurs. Its Broadway run of 472 performances made it Sherwood's longest running Broadway play, and it is certain that the production could have run much longer than it did. As a result of his performance in the title role, Raymond Massey is probably more often associated with Abraham Lincoln than he is with any of his other roles, including that of Dr. Leonard Gillespie.

Abe Lincoln in Illinois opened in October, 1938, amidst tensions engendered on the one hand by the Depression which was still afflicting many areas of the country, and on the other by the strained international situation which had been developing in Europe since Hitler's rise to power in 1933. The Lincoln play found a responsive audience because, while it did not deal directly with either of these lurking problems, it was ultimately concerned with both of them. Robert Spiller calls this a play of ". . . quietly passionate patriotism";[4] but it is much more than that. It is a mirror held up to a universal type of situation which must be dealt with by a man who is essentially simple and peace-loving. He tries to follow a moderate course, but the circumstances of the situation make such a course impossible.

No other Sherwood play is so completely an individual portrait as this one. In his earlier plays, the author had been mastering the technique of using his minor characters to reinforce his characterization of major characters. In *Abe Lincoln in Illinois* the technique has been thoroughly mastered and is skillfully used. No character in the play is seen except in relation to Lincoln; no character other than Lincoln is developed unless such development becomes a significant part of the growth of the protagonist. This technique accounts for the completely one-sided development, for instance, of Mary Todd Lincoln and of Ninian Edwards, both of whom are more fully developed than the other supporting characters in the play.

The play is in three acts and in twelve consecutively numbered scenes. The first act is concerned with Abe's early days in New Salem where he was postmaster and from whence he went to Springfield as an assemblyman. Lincoln is portrayed in this act as a hard-working young man, deeply in debt and eager to learn. His homespun philosophy is evident, as is his ability to deal with men. The second act deals with Lincoln after he has gone to Springfield and become a lawyer. During this act he meets and promises to marry Mary Todd, only to spurn her on their wedding day. However, after a considerable lapse of time, he does marry this woman whose ambition is that she one day be the wife of the President of the United States. Lincoln's simplicity is emphasized in this act, and his balanced views on slavery are enunciated. Act three is concerned with Lincoln as he takes part in the debates with Douglas, becomes the presidential candidate and ultimately the victor in the presidential contest, and finally as he boards the train to leave Springfield for Washington. The total time spanned by the play is about thirty years—a time span which would have been more difficult to handle had the Lincoln story not already been so well known to audiences.

Sherwood's task in presenting this somewhat allegorical play was made a bit less difficult than it would have been had he set out to create a hero on a purely fictional basis. Everyone who saw the play came into the theater with a sufficient store of knowledge regarding Lincoln to supply the information necessary for the unwritten fourth act, Lincoln's presidency, and fifth act, Lincoln's death at the hands of an assassin. Audiences supplied the conclusion; and, indeed, because they were so fully aware of the conclusion, because the spirit of John Wilkes Booth was always lurking darkly in the minds of audiences, the irony of many of Lincoln's lines is greatly heightened and the dramatic tension is all-pervasive.

In his parting from Springfield, the pall of impending death is very much upon him. Billy Herndon reports that Lincoln has said to him, "If I live, I'll be back some time, and then we'll go right on practising . . ."* (180). And his sister-in-law, Elizabeth Todd Edwards, replies "He's always saying that—'If I live' . . ." (180). At the very beginning of the play, the maudlin side of Lincoln's nature is revealed when Mentor Graham asks him, "You think a lot about death, don't you?" and Lincoln answers him, "I've had to, because it has always seemed to be so close to me—always—as far back as I can remember" (11). Graham gives Lincoln a copy of John Keats's "On Death" to read; and Lincoln, thirty years later, is still much aware of the poem, as Mary Lincoln indicates in saying, ". . . He had some poem in his mind, about a life of woe, along a rugged path, that leads to some future doom, and it has been an obsession with him" (147).

Sherwood's deep personal devotion to Lincoln, one which undoubtedly had about it a sense of the loneliness of the very tall man, was a partial motivation to the author in his decision to write this play. He was further moved by his warm friendship with Carl Sandburg. It was vital to Sherwood that this play should be a commercial success, for it was to be the first offering of the new Playwrights' Producing Company in which he had been a moving spirit. He wanted the play to be more than biography; he wanted it to represent his stand on a major and current social and political issue—how to deal with the spread of Fascism. Lincoln was his perfect protagonist for the accomplishment of this wish, for Lincoln was a common man faced with a huge problem involving thousands of human lives. Lincoln did not wish to make decisions. He ". . . was scared of people" (11), and he had none of the characteristics of the polished campaigner. But he was forced to take a positive stand on moral grounds. Lincoln was fully representative of what Sherwood referred to in his Postscript to *Idiot's Delight* as ". . . the decent people [who] don't want war."[5]

---

*All references are to the first edition of the play (New York: Charles Scribner's Sons, 1939).

Lincoln was also the symbol of the common man caught in the dilemma of having events antithetical to the aims of human liberty close in upon him. In Sherwood's mind, and increasingly in the minds of the people, it was no longer tenable to place peace before liberty, and *Abe Lincoln in Illinois* represents the shift in Sherwood's thinking which the progress of Fascism in Europe made inevitable. The allegory here is subtle. The play can be taken at face value as a biographical drama. But few people seeing it in 1938 and 1939 could fail to draw conclusions regarding the similarity between Lincoln's plight in 1861 and that facing the free world just prior to World War II. *Abe Lincoln in Illinois* was Sherwood's first obvious step in rejecting total pacifism. He still makes abundantly clear the fact that war is a horrible and barbaric means of settling differences; but he considers it yet a greater barbarism for men to avoid fighting in behalf of liberty when it is threatened with annihilation.

Lincoln is a compelling protagonist to use in a literary production. Like the traditional hero, his origin is vague—legends still persist that he was the illegitimate son of a Georgia plantation owner, even though such legends have been historically discounted; he has reached a high position through his own efforts and ingenuity; his life has been touched by sorrow almost to the point that Lincoln's legend is melodramatic; and he ultimately becomes the hero-martyr. As hero, Lincoln is warm, humorous at times, sincere, and infinitely human. It is Lincoln's humanity that Sherwood capitalizes on in this play. As President-elect, Lincoln is no less humble than he had been back in New Salem; he is merely more grave and has about him a greater sense of destiny. He goes forth to occupy a position which must be filled with honor and dedication. He leaves behind him all thought of ever again enjoying the privacy which he so much desires. Harris insightfully notes that Lincoln's ". . . major decision in the seventh scene does not resolve a romantic emotional problem but rather initiates the man's commitment to national issues."[6]

In none of Sherwood's previous plays had the supporting characters been merely roughed in so much as in *Abe Lincoln in Illinois*. Every character is overshadowed by the imposing Lincoln. Sherwood does not allow himself to expand on such interesting matters as Mary Todd's real feelings when Lincoln spurned her, for to do so would be to detract audience attention from the protagonist. The development of Mary Todd's character is handled with directness, verbal economy, and obvious mastery. Lincoln's future wife is first introduced in scene four where Ninian Edwards talks about her and prepares the way for her entrance into the action of the play in scene five, in which she determines to be wife to Mr. Lincoln because she is convinced that he has a brilliant future. Her calculation and determination are apparent as soon as she enters the scene. She is a clever and self-assured woman who can tell her brother-in-law, ". . . he [Lincoln] is coming to call this evening, and he will ask humbly for my hand in marriage; and, after I have displayed the proper amount of surprise and confusion, I shall murmur, timidly, 'Yes!'" (85). Her reasons for wishing to marry Abe Lincoln are very clear to her, and she says, "I simply feel that of all the men I've ever known, he is the one whose life and destiny I want most to share" (86).

There is little indication at first that Mary Todd is in love with Lincoln, and it is doubtful, indeed, that she is until his spurning her has made him seem very appealing and challenging. As she is first presented, Mary Todd is a woman of strong will and unbridled spirit. But she has a power obsession which grows through the years. She craves recognition and love; and, when she does not receive them, her resentment builds to pathological proportions. Her hysterical fit on election night is used effectively to indicate this. Actually the preparation for this fit comes somewhat earlier in scene ten when she first nags her son for smoking in the parlor, only to be humored and somewhat dismissed by her husband. Then she discovers that a committee is coming to consider Lincoln for the presidency, and she is most disturbed that she has not been told of this so that she might have had time to prepare. The final blow in this scene comes when Lincoln graciously encourages Crimmin to "Bring your seegar with you" into Mary Lincoln's dining room, when only minutes before Mary had said ". . . I shall not tolerate tobacco smoke in my parlor or, indeed, in any part of my house" (142). It is clear that Abe has always been able to make Mary aware of his feelings without engaging in outright argument with her.

Finally, strained by the tension of waiting for the election returns, Mary becomes more and more disturbed, almost to the point that one would question her sanity. She continually asks questions such as "What do they say now?" and "What are they cheering for?" (165). So tense is she that Abe finally suggests that she go home. She turns on him, wounded not just by this suggestion, but by the years of Abe's indifference which she has endured, and says, "You only want to be rid of me. That's what you've wanted ever since the day we were married—and before that. Anything to get me out of your sight, because you hate me! And it's the same with all of you—all of his friends—you hate me—you wish I'd never come into his life" (166). And constantly in the background is the fact that it was Mary Todd who turned Abe Lincoln into presidential timber. But now she has second thoughts and wistfully says, "This is the night when I'm waiting to hear that my husband has become President of the United States. And even if he does—it's ruined, for me. It's too late . . ." (167-68).

There is great pathos in the character of Mary Todd Lincoln. But Sherwood does no more than hint at this pathos, for to do more than that would be to divert attention from Lincoln himself. The final culmination of Mary's tension is used to make Lincoln seem the more lonely. He has no one to whom he can turn for real understanding. He faces the most difficult task in his country, and he faces it alone and unhappy. To a degree Mrs. Lincoln estranges him from his friends and his temperament estranges him from Mrs. Lincoln. When he is declared victor in the election and the mobs are howling for a word from him, he withdraws, emotionally spent, for he is still afraid of people as he was in the first scene in New Salem. He tells his intimates, "No, I don't want to go out there. I—I guess I'll be going on home, to tell Mary" (175). A sense of obligation leads him to go home to tell Mary, not a feeling of love for her. And this is consistent with the Lincoln personality as Sherwood portrays it: Lincoln is always moved by a sense of obligation rather than by a spontaneous yielding to his emotions. He forces himself to overcome the basic shyness of his personality and to enter politics. And he proceeds to each political task with a sense of obligation to which he becomes more pessimistically resigned through the years. There is always the sense in the play that

Lincoln is just living out his life—almost as Alan Squier was in *The Petrified Forest*. Squier feels a philosophical tie to the Petrified Forest; Lincoln feels an emotional one to the dead, and death is constantly in the forefront of his mind.

The beginning of scene ten provides skillful preparation for what is to follow. Lincoln is telling his children the story of his having to go for the doctor when Seth Gale's son was very ill (Scene VII). He tells his son Tad, ". . . the roads weren't much good then . . . and it was hard to find my way in the darkness. . . . I was afraid I'd get lost, and the boy would die, and it would be all my fault. But, finally, I found the doctor. He was very tired, and wanted to go to bed, and he grumbled a lot, but I made him come along with me then and there" (141-42). The general spirit of this speech parallels the national situation. The nation is ill with the problems of slavery and secession. Lincoln has to find his way through darkness, and he is afraid that he will lose the way, that the nation will die, and that it will be his fault. The sense of responsibility expressed in these lines which Sherwood gives to Lincoln is awesome and, indeed, burdensome. There is also the overtone that, when Lincoln finds the solution, it will not be an easy one. The citizenry will grumble, but he will force the outcome and save the nation.

Scene nine relies more on historical records than any other scene in the play. A static and formalized scene, it is a very effective one, for it presents one of the highly interesting Lincoln-Douglas debates. Lincoln is shown at his oratorical best, and his opposition is represented as being formidable. The essential moderateness of Lincoln's stand is emphasized in the long speech which Lincoln delivers. In this scene, Lincoln is presented as the developed political spokesman. Nearly twenty years have passed since the end of the preceding scene, and the transition is made swiftly and dramatically by presenting the formalized debate scene at this point.

The resolution of the great emotional crisis in Lincoln's life, which occurred just before his scheduled marriage to Mary Todd, is handled with deftness. Lincoln resists marriage to Mary Todd, presumably because she represents what he most fears but stands most in awe of: duty. Abe realizes his duty, and perhaps his destiny. But the pioneer in Abe is not dead.

It is only by a fluke that he did not leave Illinois to go to Nebraska with his friend, Seth Gale. Had he done so, it is doubtful that Lincoln would ever have been President. But on the day that he is to marry, Lincoln is faced with the possibility of turning his back on ever being able to live the life of a pioneer. Mary Todd is not the pioneering type. She is ambitious, she has been used to wealth and comfort, and she will constantly goad Abe to go east to Washington rather than west to Nebraska. Abe is especially meditative on his scheduled wedding day because his friend Bowling Green has on that very day been buried, and Bowling Green represents for Abe that period of his life when Anne Rutledge died. Abe cannot go through with the ceremony and leaves Springfield.

However, after he has spent some time wandering around, Abe again meets his friend, Seth Gale, who with his family is now headed for the frontier. After his reunion with these people, Abe realizes his destiny, for Seth talks about the advance of slavery and tells Abe "That territory [Oregon] has got to be free! If this country ain't strong enough to protect its citizens from slavery, then we'll cut loose from it and join with Canada. Or, better yet, we'll make a *new* country out there in the far west" (119). Abe now states his mission: ". . . seeing you now— and thinking of the big thing you've set out to do—well, it's made me feel pretty small. It's made me feel that I've got to do something, too, to keep you and your kind in the United States of America" (120). And after this scene, Abe takes the all-important step toward shaping his destiny by returning to Springfield to marry Miss Todd.

John Mason Brown pinpoints one of the severe dramatic limitations in *Abe Lincoln in Illinois* in his contention that ". . . Mr. Sherwood leaves out most of his illustrative action."[7] It is true that Lincoln's development is not dramatized for the audience; rather it happens between scenes. For example, between scenes eight and nine, as has been mentioned, about twenty years elapse, and Lincoln has grown from the uncertain, hypochondriacal young lawyer to the presidential hopeful who is engaged in a debate with Stephen A. Douglas. Mr. Brown in regard to this specific part of the play notes that "Mr. Sherwood does not prepare us for Lincoln's greatness. His greatness overtakes him during an intermission."[8] It is very true that Sherwood sometimes took undue advantage of the fact that audiences were already aware of Lincoln's stature and did not set out to illustrate that which he considered to be known and popularly accepted. From a dramatic point of view, this is a weakness; and, as has been mentioned previously,[9] this flaw is not confined to the present play alone. It pervaded *The Petrified Forest* in a way which Mr. Lawson has carefully detailed in *The Theory and Technique of Playwriting*.[10] It is also true that Harry Van's returning to Irene and Hannibal's turning from the gates of Rome are events which are stated rather than developed; and the result is that the events are less convincing than they might ideally have been.

It is important to recognize that Sherwood had lifted his sights in *Abe Lincoln in Illinois* from individual sacrifice on a one-to-one ratio—as seen, for example, in Alan Squier's dying so that Gabby might lead a fuller life or in Harry Van's sacrifice in returning to Irene—to the plane on which the individual makes a sacrifice for a more general good. Squier's death and Van's presumed one are depicted as examples of personal nobility; however, society is not significantly altered by their acts and sacrifices. Lincoln, on the other hand, makes a personal sacrifice for the general good, for the benefit of his nation whose solidarity is being threatened, and his act is memorable and meaningful in broadly historic terms. Lincoln is the man of action who has been denied in Sherwood's previous works. If Hannibal fell under the spell of Amytis' words and charms and if Alan Squier and Harry Van denied action in preference to an abstract idealism, Lincoln, in complete contradistinction to these three protagonists, was driven to action by the force of words and events. And action in the cause of freedom becomes an ultimate moral good when a peaceful solution is not tenable.

Joseph Wood Krutch contends that the play ". . . was romantic as much as it was didactic";[11] this is so in regard to the characterization, especially of the protagonist. However, the play's theme is clearly didactic rather than romantic. And this didacticism grows as the author works out his philosophical stand in regard to man's responsibility to protect freedom in *There Shall Be No Night* and *The Rugged Path*. In *The Petrified Forest* and in *Idiot's Delight* romanticism and didacticism are united in the presentation of theme; the very nature of both of these plays makes this a dramatic necessity. But the intent of the Lincoln play excluded romanticism from the thematic development. Walter P. Eaton wrote that "What Sherwood most wished to tell, I think, is summed up in a sentence Speed wrote to Herndon. 'He must believe he was right, and that he had truth and justice with him, or he was a weak man; but no man could be stronger if he thought he was right.' To show us the weak Lincoln, to show us the gradual infiltration of a belief in the truth and justice of the cause he was called on to lead . . . was Mr. Sherwood's task."[12] If there is any doubt about the didacticism of *Abe Lincoln in Illinois*, the ending of the play should dispel it. The curtain falls with the crowd which has come to bid Lincoln farewell singing "John Brown's Body." The play ends as they reach the line "His soul goes marching on"—as striking an example of dramatic didacticism as one can find.

The Lincoln play is the first production which Sherwood really approached with a feeling of awesome respect and virtual reverence. The result is that many of the devices of his earlier plays, which the critics labeled "hokum," are not present. Sherwood took definite shortcuts in this play, but he depended upon the audience to bridge the gaps, which he left, with its specific knowledge of Lincoln and Civil War history which most of them brought to the performance of the play.

III   There Shall Be No Night

In *Abe Lincoln in Illinois*, Robert Sherwood made a study of the causes of war and of the reactions of one heroic, peace-loving man to these causes. *There Shall Be No Night* also has its heroic and peace-loving man in Dr. Kaarlo Valkonen, a neurologist, a winner of the Nobel Peace Prize, a man whose profession has made him more an internationalist than a narrow patriot. But this play is concerned much more with effects than with specific, narrow causes and with the reaction of the pacifist scientist to these effects. History had made known to every schoolboy the effects of the Civil War; in the Lincoln play, Sherwood chose to concentrate his attention upon some of the causes. But the daily news media at the time that Sherwood was writing *There Shall Be No Night* were blaring the causes of the European conflict to the public at large, and the total effects were really not finally written until 1945.

Kaarlo Valkonen lives in Helsinki with his wife, Miranda, and their teen-age son, Erik. Miranda, an American from New Bedford, Massachusetts, is a descendant of an old American family whose portraits decorate the walls of the Valkonen living room, along with pictures of Pavlov, Freud, the Mayo brothers, and others notable in scientific areas related to Dr. Valkonen's. So accustomed has Miranda become to living in Finland for the past twenty-odd years that she can conceive of no place else as home.

The play opens on the day that Dr. Valkonen is to make a trans-Atlantic broadcast about having been awarded the Nobel Prize. The atmosphere is happy and light; there is much banter and the sense is conveyed that the Valkonens rank high among the world's civilized, cultivated, contributing citizens. Their home-life is ideal, as is well shown through the reaction of Dave Corween, the American newsman who introduces Dr. Valkonen to the radio audience, to this pleasant household. The only discordant note in the scene is the urgent realization by the principals that Czechoslovakia and Poland have recently fallen to the Nazis. Erik and his fiancé, Kaatri, are especially aware of what might be impending. They have been working on the Mannerheim Line, and Kaatri especially, being the daughter of a military man, views the situation realistically and fears that Finland's days are numbered. What follows confirms Kaatri's fears, and she, indeed, of all the principals, is the only one to escape from Finland. Erik is to go off to the war as a ski-trooper, Kaarlo is to go to Viipuri to minister to wounded soldiers at the front, Miranda and Uncle Waldemar are to remain at home; but all are to die—Erik and Kaarlo before the play ends, and Miranda and Uncle Waldemar, presumably, shortly after it ends.

Nevertheless, in purely universal terms, the play is a hopeful one. Sherwood writes into it suggestions of continuance. Kaatri goes to the safety of America to have Erik's baby and this, as Miranda tells Dave Corween, ". . . means one little link with the future. It gives us the illusion of survival—and perhaps it isn't just an illusion" * (140). And in a broader sense, Dr. Valkonen

---

*All references are to the first edition of the play (New York: Charles Scribner's Sons, 1940).

in his speech to America quoted Jung as saying "There is no coming to consciousness without pain" (22). The implication is quite clear: the world is moving toward consciousness, and the present strife is a part of this motion. Dr. Valkonen is also fond of quoting St. Paul's words, "We glory in tribulations; knowing that tribulation worketh patience; and patience, experience; and experience, hope" (176).

And in the name of hope, Sherwood for the first time clearly lets it be known that his thinking of the early and middle 1930's has shifted and that he would now have men fight to preserve freedom. Gosden, the British pacifist whom Valkonen and his American ambulance drivers come upon in a remote Finnish schoolhouse, states very clearly what has now come to be Sherwood's credo: "Every one of us can find plenty of reasons for *not* fighting, and they're the best reasons in the world. But— the time comes when you've bloody well got to fight—and you might just as well go cheerfully" (162).

There is also hope in the work to which Dr. Valkonen has devoted his life. He has been concerned with neurological and psychological research. He has said in his broadcast to America, ". . . I think the Nobel prize is premature. The work I am doing will be finished by some one else many years from now" (19). And throughout the play Valkonen emphasizes that his work is a mere beginning and that it might take hundreds of years to complete it. He also, late in the play, tells what war is: "All of this—reasonless war—it's a psychological epidemic" (151). And if Valkonen's work is in the direction of making men more rational, which it clearly seems to be, then the epidemic can eventually be wiped out. Throughout the more crucial parts of the action, Sherwood has characters say such things as "They are coming to consciousness" (152), and "That is consciousness" (153). And there are constant echoes of Valkonen's quotation from Jung early in the play: "There is no coming to consciousness without pain."

Furthermore, in the preface to *Reunion in Vienna,* from which Sherwood quotes extensively in the preface to *There Shall Be No Night,* he presents a clear indication of his thinking along these lines; but in this preface he is not nearly so hopeful as he is in *There Shall Be No Night.* He writes: "This is the career of the age of reason: The eighteenth century knew the excitements of conception, culminating in the supreme orgasm of the French Revolution. The nineteenth century was the period of gestation, marred by occasional symptoms of nausea and hysteria and a few dark forebodings, but generally orderly and complacent. For the twentieth century have remained the excruciating labor pains and the discovery that the child is a monster; and as a modern man looks upon it, and recalls the assurances of the omniscient obstetricians, he is sore distressed" (xvii). *Reunion in Vienna* was written, according to Sherwood, as an escape from thinking about things that troubled him, and some of these things are mentioned in his preface to the play.

By the time he came to write *There Shall Be No Night*, there was no means by which he could escape from the things which troubled him and the whole of society. But now his means of escape was to be found in his tenuous offering of hope. Joseph Wood Krutch speculates that ". . . his present concern with specific political issues is as much an 'escape' from deeper questions too puzzling to think about as *Reunion in Vienna* was an escape from the relatively more serious things even then struggling in his mind for recognition."[13] This may be true in part, but philosophically the Sherwood of *There Shall Be No Night* had grappled with the large problems which perplexed his soul, and he had reached a solution to them. This solution is the conditional sort of pacifism found in his play about the Finnish plight. More than half the major characters in the play are philosophically pacifist: Dr. Valkonen; Erik, who scornfully calls Alfred Nobel "the dynamite king" (31); Miranda, whose pacifism is based mostly on wanting to preserve her family; Gosden, the English pacifist; and Frank Olmstead, the American ambulance driver.

Dr. Valkonen may easily be taken at face value in the play; however, his symbolic value is also evident. *Time Magazine's* critic wrote that Sherwood's ". . . pacifist who, after studying the issues at stake, decides to fight can easily be taken as a symbol: Sherwood might well wish an anti-war U.S. to change its mind as Valkonen did."[14] Sherwood denied the suggestion that he was calling for American intervention in the war; however, such denials ring rather false in view of various elements in the present play. First, the audience is told that America has offered to mediate the difficulties between Finland and

Russia—certainly a diplomatic intervention. Secondly, Sherwood very pointedly involves Americans in the Finnish crisis in the persons of the ambulance drivers. But even more important than these means of showing that America is drawn into the conflict indirectly, Sherwood gives some very tacit criticism of America in two specific incidents. To begin with, when Kaarlo was testing the microphone prior to his trans-Atlantic broadcast, he was asked just to say anything into it so that the controls might be adjusted to his voice. He says, ". . . do you know that the human digestive tract or alimentary canal extends for a distance of twenty-five or thirty feet, and consists of the following main parts: the mouth, pharnyx, œsophagus, stomach, small intestines, cæcum, large intestines, rectum and anus? . . ." (4). Miranda reacts to this in a typically American way: "Now, Kaarlo—when you do speak to the American people, please don't forget yourself and go through all those disgusting organs again. People don't like to be reminded of such things" (5).

This speech in itself might not be very telling; however, it correlates with something that Kaatri says in the following scene: "What good is his [Erik's] life if it has to be spent in slavery? And that's what it would be if he gave in to them. Slavery for you—for all of us. Oh, I know that you Americans don't like to think of such terrible things" (54). And Kaatri follows this utterance with a statement that "When life becomes too easy for people, something changes in their character, something is lost. Americans now are too lucky. In your blood is the water of those oceans that have made your country safe" (56).

The burden of what is said here is that it would be not only ignoble, but demoralizing to the United States for her not to take a stand. In a very real sense, Sherwood uses Mrs. Valkonen to represent the United States. He notes her fondness for making a good appearance and her tendency to feign frivolity. She has not the youthful zeal and intensity of Kaatri. Her interests are essentially centered in her home. But she will not turn her back on the situation which befalls Finland. Rather, she faces the certain loss of everything she possesses, including her life, in order to remain and preserve the ideals for which and by which she has always lived.

The greatest irony in the play is that of Sherwood's own shift in position through the years of international tension. This shift is compressed into two or three months in the life of Kaarlo Valkonen. He is the man of peace not only in his own heart, but also in the eyes of the world. He has been awarded a prize which is designated for those who advance the cause of peace in the world. The entire civilized world knows that he is a man of peace. He is also a man who essentially is beyond the narrow limits of patriotism, and he realizes this, for he tells Dave Corween "I'm not a patriotic citizen of this country, Mr. Corween. I hope I am aware of the fact that 'patriotism' as now practiced is one of the most virulent manifestations of evil" (79). And Corween answers, "You're a citizen of the world. You're of importance to the whole world, not just to these few gallant men who are going to fight and die for Finland."

But Valkonen is drawn into the conflict because of his great humanity. He cannot see wounded Finnish boys go unattended; so he leaves his home and goes into the front lines, unarmed, to alleviate suffering. And, in doing so, he is still acting consistently; he is still the pacifist rendering emergency service to those direly in need of it. Even on the battlefield, Valkonen remains essentially the medical researcher. He tells Frank Olmstead, "I think I've learned a great deal in the last few months. Research work in the field! I never dreamed I would have such a vast laboratory, with so many specimens. . . . It is wonderful to see what men are capable of—what courage— what endurance—what utter lack of selfishness. And what a tragedy that these heroic qualities can be tested only by disease" (150-51).

However, the final retreat comes. In an isolated schoolhouse, faced by almost certain death, Valkonen discusses his book, *The Defense of Man*, with Frank Olmstead. In this schoolhouse he is given a revolver and belt. He puts on the belt as a signification of his final decision. He will fight to the death the inroads which aggression makes upon human liberty. Frank rues the situation. He says that Valkonen's book advocates that "The true defenses of man are *in* man, himself." He goes on to say, "So now—there's nothing left for the great thinker to do but take a gun and go up there and shoot" (160).

Valkonen's own letter, delivered after his death to Miranda, tells generally what the death of one man means in the cause of freedom: ". . . Erik and the others who give their lives are also giving to mankind a symbol—a little symbol, to be sure, but a clear one—of man's unconquerable aspiration to dignity and freedom and purity in the sight of God" (176). This letter, based largely upon the philosophy of Pericles' *Funeral Oration* and adapted from Sherwood's earlier pacifist play, *Acropolis*, is the author's call to arms. It is not a call based upon a broadly patriotic appeal. Rather, it is a goad to man's conscience, an idealistic nudge toward the preservation of human dignity and freedom for all time.

Sherwood's sentiments about the impersonality of war, manifested early in *Waterloo Bridge* where Roy tells Myra, "Just think of the old guy up there [the pilot of a bomber] with eight million people to aim at" (*ed. cit.*, 37), are repeated by Miranda in virtually the same way that they appear in *Waterloo Bridge*. She is suggesting that her husband might be killed if she accepts an offer to flee from Finland without him. He cannot conceive of being killed and says, "I am a doctor," to which Miranda answers, almost as Roy might have, but with much less optimism, "And do you suppose a Russian in a bombing plane ten thousand feet up can tell the difference between an ordinary person and a winner of the Nobel prize?" (94-95). Indeed, in modern warfare an ironic perversion of the democratic ideal has been reached: all men are equal—equal in their insignificance to those dropping the bombs or pushing the firing buttons.

Dr. Ziemssen is the German Consul in Helsinki. A well-trained anthropologist turned Nazi apologist, Ziemssen has as much regard for Dr. Valkonen as one can who has ceased to believe in the dignity of man. He comes to the Valkonen household to try to persuade Kaarlo to leave Helsinki before it is too late. This interview in scene three is very interesting from several standpoints. To begin with, the relationship of Nazism to Communism is clearly and undiplomatically stated by Ziemssen. This relationship has moved several steps since Odets' *Till the Day I Die*, for the Russians and Germans are now allies. But Ziemssen reveals the basis of this alliance when he says to Kaarlo, "We make good use of our esteemed allies of the Soviet Union. . . . Communism is a good laxative to loosen the constricted bowels of democracy. When it has served that purpose, it will disappear down the sewer with the excrement that must be purged" (86). Ziemssen clearly states the Nazi plan for the future: "This is a process of annihilation. It is a studied technique, and it was not invented in Moscow. You will find the blueprints of it, not in *Das Kapital*, but in *Mein Kampf.* . . . It involves, first, liquidation of all leaders of thought—political, religious, economic, intellectual. Among the masses—the difficult ones are killed—the weaklings are allowed to die of starvation—the strong ones are enslaved" (87).

Here, of course, Sherwood is at his most propagandistically forceful. Nothing could more fully arouse a tense, apprehensive, frightened, hating public than such a statement, and Sherwood realized it. The greatest rub is that Ziemssen, *an anthropologist,* should ignore what he knows to be genetically true, and should dismiss any consideration of conscience by saying, "Naturally, I regret the necessity for it. But I *admit* the necessity." And here, indeed, Sherwood vindicates himself for having abandoned his stand of absolute pacifism. Pacifism is tenable only among people of conscience. All that Kaarlo believes and has devoted his life to—scientific truth—Ziemssen in an instant denies, using as his explanation racial superiority. He tells Kaarlo, "Of course it is a lie, biologically [the idea of racism]. But we can prove it by the very simple expedient of asserting our own superiority" (88). And now, to an audience already aroused, Sherwood has Ziemssen say that America for the time is secure, as long as she does not hamper the Nazi plans for Mexico, South America, and Canada. And of the Americans he says, "They are learning to mind their own shrinking business" (89). If this is not a direct call to action and intervention, the stage has never seen one.

Ziemssen serves the purpose not only of arousing audiences but also of representing the antithesis of Dr. Valkonen. The total implication is clear. Ziemssen, significant of all that is base, scientifically dishonest, and self-seeking in society, is on the side of the strong. Valkonen, clearly aligned with the side of good, is now on the side of the physically weak—two-hundred-thousand men against ten-million—and is bound to go down in defeat, carrying with him his priceless ideals and, indeed, the hope of humanity. The fight will be an equable one only if the sides are more evenly matched, and only American intervention can assure that they will be.

The play contains a subplot which has been criticized adversely by some newspaper critics. This subplot is concerned with the romance between the Valkonens' son, Erik, and Kaatri. However, it must be noted that this subplot serves a number of significant purposes. In the first place, the introduction of Kaatri is significant, because she represents a family completely opposite in outlook to the Valkonen family by the very fact that her father has been a military man all his life. Secondly, Kaatri is as much the antithesis of Miranda, as Dr. Ziemssen is of Dr. Valkonen. The Valkonens' reactions to Kaatri do much to indicate their stature and great humanity. When Miranda is told that Kaatri is pregnant by their son to whom she is not married, Miranda responds with utter sincerity, "Darling" (126), and takes Kaatri into her arms.

But the most significant element of the subplot is that it emphasizes perhaps the most horrible reality of war: the futility which young people are made to feel and to endure because of it. When hope should be highest, death beclouds the future of the upcoming generation. Adulthood is thrust ruthlessly and hastily upon the adolescent, and in the short hours before his death, he is forced to experience all of life—at least all that remains for him. The pathos of this situation is universally felt and has come to represent, even today, one of the greatest dislocations of the age.

There Shall Be No Night is a deeply moving play. Many of Sherwood's earlier plays, notably *The Petrified Forest* and *Idiot's Delight*, faltered severely at the end. However, in both *Abe Lincoln in Illinois* and *There Shall Be No Night* the endings are very skillfully conceived dramatically. Miranda's reading of Kaarlo's final letter to Dave Corween brings the play full circle. The implications of Kaarlo's letter are implications for all mankind: a latter day Periclean *Funeral Oration*. If hope is not implicit in all that the letter states, human purpose is. The ending of the play, pervaded by the Finnish folk melody which Uncle Waldemar is playing on the piano, is peopled with the ghosts of Kaarlo and Erik. The stage directions say that Miranda ". . . looks to the left, where Erik had been, and to the right, where Kaarlo had been" (178). And the Finnish melody reinforces a fragment of hope which Kaarlo gives in the schoolhouse scene shortly before his death. He notices that around the walls of the schoolroom are inscriptions of verses from the

Kalevala, the epic poem of Finland. And he tells his American friend, Frank Olmstead, "It [the *Kalevala*] had its beginnings in the songs of our minstrels a thousand years ago" (148). Through a thousand years of trials, Finland had endured with honor; and the implication that she will continue to survive is clear both in what Kaarlo has said and in the fact that Erik's baby will be born in the safety of the New World and will carry with him the ideals which generations of his family have preserved.

There Shall Be No Night was more than a popular play: it was a play which represented a mission on the part of both the author and the Lunts who played the leading roles. In the middle of the war the Lunts made the dangerous trans-Atlantic journey to London to present the play amid the wreckage of the sorely battered British capital. And in London, "By a deft rewriting of the play, which set the locale in Greece instead of in Finland, with German aggressors instead of Russians, it became just as topical and *apropos* as an indictment of the Fascist brand of tyranny as it was against the Communist brand."[15]

Few people, including Sherwood himself, would call *There Shall Be No Night* great art. It is doubtful that propaganda can ever qualify as such, since its chief concern is not artistic and since it is usually too topical to capitalize fully on the artistic possibilities of a situation. Be that as it may, the Sherwood offering was more significantly artistic than such anti-Nazi plays of the same period as Elmer Rice's *Flight to the West*, Maxwell Anderson's *Candle in the Wind*, Lillian Hellman's *Watch on the Rhine*, Clifford Odets' *Till the Day I Die*, or Clare Boothe Luce's *Margin for Error*. Of all these plays, including Sherwood's, one might say what Grenville Vernon said of *There Shall Be No Night*: the authors were too close to the situation which had no time to ". . . pass through the fires of [their] imagination [but only through] the flames of [their] indignation."[16]

Joseph Wood Krutch, who compares this play with *The Petrified Forest* and *Idiot's Delight*, calls it ". . . an exciting thesis melodrama." He continues to say that ". . . actuality has sobered a playwright plainly too deeply concerned to contrive merely theatrical effects. [The play] is palpably sincere, frequently touching, and occasionally exciting, [but] one leaves the theatre with the sense that the play has not really risen to the subject."[17] He goes on to call the play diffuse, and he very correctly points out that it "nowhere gathers itself together in climax . . . one is perpetually waiting for the scene that never comes." But he notes the source of Sherwood's chief difficulty in *There Shall Be No Night,* a source which Sherwood himself admits in his preface to the play: ". . . his play is less dramatic than a year of radio and newspaper." All of the playwrights who chose to write topically of the international situation were beset by this difficulty. Krutch calls Sherwood's philosophical failure a ". . . part of the general failure of civilized and reflective mankind."

The play was popular with audiences largely because, as Nannes notes in *Politics in the American Drama,* "Sherwood was in tune with the country when he wrote the drama."[18] Ira Wolfert wrote in the Washington *Evening Star*[19] that "Mr. Sherwood has not been a leader of thought, nor has he gone off on tangents of his own. His plays are popular. Their meaning is accepted by large audiences. He has been neither dead, nor behind, nor away from the life with which he has been surrounded."

This opinion is certainly seconded by John Mason Brown who calls Sherwood ". . . a lean-to in the field of the theatre [rather] than . . . a self-reliant dramatist."[20] But Brown also notes that if *There Shall Be No Night* is static, it ". . . is at least becalmed in the interest of good talk . . . [and] proves absorbing for by far the better portion of one of the season's most arresting and moving evenings."[21]

Rosamond Gilder considered the play one which explains the survival of the theater and "justifies the faith of those who see in it one of the highest forms of human expression."[22] Dr. Valkonen's death becomes a highly generalized and meaningful sacrifice. He does not, as Harris concludes, ". . . die for the love of his fellow man."[23] He dies for something much fuller and far-reaching than that: for concepts. He dies for the preservation of human dignity, in the very real hope that man can conquer bestiality ". . . with the power of the light that is in our minds" (153).

IV The Rugged Path

The outcome of *The Rugged Path* is foretold in the title, which is taken from Keats's "On Death." The lines from which the title is derived read:

> How strange it is that men on earth should roam,
> And lead a life of woe, but not forsake
> His rugged path—nor dare he view alone
> His future doom—which is but to awake.

Morey Vinion's "rugged path" led him to abandon his position as editor to take an active part in World War II, first as a cook in the United States Navy, and later, after the sinking of his ship near the Philippine Islands, as the commander of a guerrilla task force.

The Rugged Path was originally intended to be two separate plays.[24] The merging of these two plays into the present product was painful and was never wholly successful. Lewis Nichols was correct in his judgment in the New York *Times* that "The approach to the first [act] is intellectual; the second is more active."[25] The unifying devices which Sherwood used to effect the merger are contrived. The opening scene of the play, which takes place in the White House, is without any structural justification except that it gives a foretaste of the concluding scene which is also in the White House. The concluding scene is also contrived and is designed to add unity to a disunified and unfocused play. The only statement which can be made in favor of the last scene is that it has the potential for an irony suggestive of the concluding chapter of Waugh's *A Handful of Dust*. However, this potential is not developed, for Sherwood cannot sufficiently overcome his emotional involvement with his play and its problems to be anything but deadly serious and earnest until the final curtain.

Gone from this play is the lightness which softened the bitter pessimism of *Idiot's Delight* or of *Reunion in Vienna*. Sherwood had lived through a decade of painful soul-searching and agonizing decision, and *The Rugged Path* was the plaint born of these years. This protest is given words as Morey Vinion tells Dr. Querin, the Filipino philosophy professor who is now a guerrilla warrior, ". . . I am no longer impressed by the power of the pen. For years I wrote about what was coming. I tried to tell what I had seen and heard and felt. I wrote my heart out. But it did no good"* (337). This is the most totally subjective utterance that Sherwood makes in any of his plays. And these are the words of a hurt and disillusioned man. But *The Rugged Path* is painful evidence that Sherwood has abandoned one set of values, but has not really found another to replace it.

Morey, who has been a foreign correspondent and often in the thick of the battle, is called home in 1940 to be editor of the newspaper run by the Bowsmiths, his wife's family. A man used to action, he finds it impossible for various reasons to adjust to life as the editor of a publication which panders to the isolationist leanings of its advertisers while overlooking the basic *raison d'être* of a newspaper which, in Morey's eyes, involves speaking out courageously on controversial issues and in trying to direct public opinion honestly and rationally. Throughout the first act, Morey is straining to get away from the newspaper and from his lack-luster marriage. His wife, who realizes his discontent, confronts her husband with the indictment that he is no longer in love with her. He does not deny this, but rather reminds her of what her father, who before his death was the owner of the newspaper, had said to him when he and Harriet were about to marry: "You're a damned good newspaper man, Morey, which means that you'll be a damned poor husband" (314). And Morey adds, ". . . that's the way it has worked out."

When Morey finally decides to go to war, to enlist in the navy rather than to use his influence to gain a commission, he is motivated more by discontent with the newspaper and with his home life than he is by any desire to fight for humanity. Here is no Kaarlo Valkonen who would give up his life for a cause, turning his back on an assured escape to a place where he could live in honor, carry on his work, and preserve the happiness which he has known in his family situation. Here

*All references are to the only printed version of *The Rugged Path* which appears in abridged form in Burns Mantle, *Best Plays of 1945-46* (New York: Dodd, Mead and Company, Incorporated, 1946). A typescript of the play is in the New York City Public Library.

rather is a man who expresses no pacifist ideals—nor, indeed, does anyone in this play—and who wants nothing so much as to forestall the onset of middle age by engaging in activities of youth. He tells his wife that he is not the right husband for her, and the dialogue which follows reveals his true motives for wanting to get away:

HARRIET: Then joining the Navy is your means of leaving me.
MOREY: You'll be making a cruel mistake if you believe that.
HARRIET: What can I believe, Morey?
MOREY: That there's a chance that after this experience, whatever it may be, you and I will have found a way to live at peace, with each other.

(325)

The audience has already been told that Harriet and Morey have gotten along together ". . . because we both have good manners." The above scene gives ample evidence of this as well as of Morey's motivations for leaving behind him the stale world in which he finds himself.

After Morey has been in the navy for some time, he is still looking for an answer to the question of why he really joined. He suspects his motivations, but he is not quite able to admit them. He asks the doctor on his ship in the Pacific, "All these kids—this generation. Why do they fight? That kid Costanzo, for instance. He saw service in the North Atlantic against U-boats, and he's been out here in the Pacific for over a year. He and all the rest of them have no reason to believe that they'll ever get back alive. What's in their minds? What do they think they're accomplishing?" (329). But the burden of these questions is upon Morey; his real question is "Why am I doing it? What am I accomplishing?"

Morey does not find the answer to his questions until his ship is sunk and he is cast upon a small island in the Philippines where he meets the guerrilla force of which he is to become a part and with which he is to die a distinguished and heroic death for which he is awarded posthumously the Medal of Honor by the President of the United States. On this remote island, Dr. Querin pinpoints part of Morey's social dislocation when he says, "I'm afraid you have known too much, you have seen too much of the veil that is abroad in the world" (337).

And Morey, at the end of the first act, has virtually admitted as much in saying to Harriet, "The trouble is that we're both, in a way, casualties of this war" (326). The word *era,* in the context of this play, would have been a more valid one than war.

If there is a tentativeness in Sherwood's development of Morey's character, it is because there is a tentativeness in the epoch. This is an age in which the most promising youth—here represented by the one-time Rhodes scholar, Gil Hartnick, fired from Morey's paper because of his editorial supporting Winston Churchill's plea for lend-lease to Russia—must go out and die in some far removed portion of the world while at home remain the defenders of American isolationism and big business. In the first act of this play there are echoes of what Sinclair Lewis was vehemently proclaiming in the 1920's in *Babbitt* and in *Main Street* and of what Odets was declaring in the 1930's in *Waiting for Lefty* and *Golden Boy.* And this play ideologically is just one step behind the haunting specters which are to be produced in the 1940's in such plays as Arthur Miller's *Death of a Salesman* and William Inge's *Dark at the Top of the Stairs.*

The only impediment which prevented Sherwood from producing a work such as any of these was that he did not—or would not, or could not—believe in his inmost self that what he was writing about was true, or at least that it was true enough to be representative. By this time, fear of the truth lurked in Robert Sherwood's fine mind. His essential pacifism had been killed by the international events which precipitated the war, and he had found no convincing substitute for an outmoded pacifism. By 1945, he had come to consider a possibility—one which is certainly not pleasant to consider—that Dr. Querin voices for him: "I am afraid that you [Americans] will not have the courage and the wisdom to be great in times of peace as you have been in times of war" (337). And this is not a new thought with Sherwood. He had stated the germ of it five years earlier in *There Shall Be No Night.* Dr. Valkonen has expressed his admiration for what man can rise to under the pressure of battle and has said, ". . . what a tragedy that these heroic qualities can be tested only by disease [war]" (*Ed. cit.,* 151).

The necessary conclusion to be drawn from such a statement is one which is in complete opposition to Sherwood's pacifism of the 1930's. Sherwood has come to admit that man must have a

challenge in order to develop his greatest potential, but he has
not seen the challenge in anything but the extreme and generalized tension of world conflict. Like Darwin nearly a century
before, Sherwood did not like his conclusions; but he was led
to them by data which he could not reasonably doubt. Morey
Vinion's dislocation is Sherwood's dislocation; but Morey Vinion
finds the solution to his problem in a course of action which
leads to an honorable death. This course is not open to Sherwood;
but the solution haunts him continually and arouses in him the
same sort of confusion which is evident in *The Rugged Path*.

Morey Vinion is an interesting portrait of a perplexed,
thoughtful, terribly lonely man. During his editorship of the
newspaper, he lives in an atmosphere to which he is ideologically
alien. Because he is serious and responsible, the burden of fault
is often upon him. He represents the liberal view, along with
Gil Hartnick. George Bowsmith, son of the founder of the
newspaper and Morey's brother-in-law, is, in contrast not nearly
so dedicated to journalism as Morey. When world crises are
breaking, George is off fishing. He is basically a decent fellow,
but his aim in life is to avoid trouble. But this avoidance is not
always possible because he finds himself caught between the
ultra-conservatism of the paper's business manager, Leggatt
Burt, and Morey's liberalism. By tradition he casts his lot more
easily with Burt than with Morey, but he would much prefer
not to be called upon to cast his lot at all.

George has inherited his philosophical position rather than
thought it out. This is evident, for example, in the description
of his office: "It is an old-fashioned office with old-fashioned
furniture and a great many books and files in untidy arrangement" (319). This description is followed by a stage direction
that indicates that George ". . . had tried to keep it [the news-
paper] the way his dad wanted it. Even to this dreary old office"
(322). Morey is trying to fight against a dissipated memory,
and the qualifying adjective is most important. For old Mr.
Bowsmith himself was never weak and ineffectual. He had
principles and he fought to preserve them. His principles were
not Morey's, but Morey could respect the old man's sincerity
and integrity. Of the old man, Morey says: "He was a Black
Republican. He was a product of the Robber Baron era. He
believed in the doctrine of every man for himself. But he was

an American—and a fighter. There were giants in the land in those days" (318). But now Morey tells George ruefully, "The dead hand is heavy" (323).

Echoes from *The Petrified Forest* are strong here. Just as Gramp Maples and Alan Squier rued the passing of the pioneer— the death of the ultimate individualist—so does Morey remember with nostalgia a fiercely dedicated man with whom he had generally disagreed. George Bowsmith is not a challenge to Morey as the old man was, for George does not have ideas or ideals of his own. Leggatt Burt takes a firmer stand than George, but he takes his stand because he wants to mollify his advertisers, not because he believes in something. Morey Vinion comes home from a field of action in wartime England to a stronghold of inaction in his own community. The meaning of life is nullified for him while he is there. If he does not love his wife and his townfolk and his home and his job so much as he should after an absence of some years, it is because he has been so appalled by what he has returned to that he has built a psychological wall between it and himself. He has insulated himself so that he will be able to bear it by feeling it less. He grapples in the no man's land between duty and self-fulfillment, and he makes the only choice possible to one whose values are what his are. The war for Morey Vinion, as for so many, provided a base from which he could fight his way toward fulfillment. He could not communicate his real motives for joining the navy, largely because he was not fully aware of them himself. Possibly Harriet has a faint understanding of them when she asks Dr. Querin to take Morey's Medal of Honor back to the Philippines.

Morey was more fortunate than most, for he escaped from that which he could no longer live with and he found something which he could live with. After his ship has been sunk, he says, "Home? When I think of home . . . I think of a little tin-can that now lies broken to pieces on the bottom of the Pacific. And all my folks, all my own people, are down there, dead" (337). In other words, Morey has turned his back upon men of inaction to cast his lot with those who through their action bring about their own deaths. He has not turned his back in bitterness, for he has found something to replace that which he has rejected. He has, one must presume, merely forgotten that there was a life for him before he left the newspaper and became a strong individual.

In death, his own and those of the people he had most come to cherish, Morey found life. He tells the audience this in so many words: ". . . the men and women of the *Mayflower*, and the Alamo, and the covered wagons. I thought they were gone and forgotten. . . . I've found them here . . . I've known them and I've seen them, living and fighting. And what this has meant to me is beyond measurement, beyond expression. It's a revival of the spirit—a restoration of faith—the discovery of life" (338). And then, in essence, he states the sentiment of the Jungian philosophy which Dr. Valkonen enunciated in *There Shall Be No Night*: "You don't get these things free."

The Rugged Path is somewhat lacking in conflict. Presumably there is a conflict going on within Morey; however, it is never shown in any fully realized way within the play. The effects of Morey's conflict are shown, but never are the causes pinned down so dramatically as they might be. The second act particularly falls apart dramatically and becomes little more than a diatribe during which, as *Time Magazine's* reviewer noted, "The hero is sometimes protagonist, sometimes symbol, sometimes Robert E. Sherwood."[26] Harsh though this reviewer seems, most discerning audiences who saw *The Rugged Path* would have to agree with him that ". . . the play as a whole is a tangled Sherwood Forest of Ideas."[27] The ideas are fascinating to one who has traced Sherwood's evolution as a dramatist, but Sherwood's personal confusion regarding the role of the liberal in the war-torn society of 1945 intruded itself upon his play with dramatically disastrous effects.

Mr. Krutch contended that ". . . the real defect in almost all our so-called serious plays is simply that they are not in any dramatic, or poetic, or philosophical sense serious enough." And in the same review, he specifically said of *The Rugged Path* that it ". . . fails on its own level because, I think, it is merely more serious [than *Deep Are the Roots*] without really being serious enough. A play as important as the author wants this one to be would have to be founded upon some conviction too fundamental to be shaken by local events possible in the near future, upon truths which could survive mere political realignments."[28]

Sherwood's seriousness in the 1930's had the veneer of drawing room comedy about it which made it popular with audiences. His thinking was more often in the area of abstractions—peace, brotherhood, internationalism—than it could possibly be after the shock of a bloody, costly and terrifying world holocaust. Just as Sherwood had approached the memory of Lincoln with reverence, he now stood in awesome reverence of all that the war meant in terms of human life. This attitude prevented him from realizing his full dramatic potential in the writing of the play. And on stage, unfortunately, Morey Vinion became what Kappo Phelan described as ". . . a kind of true-to-life photograph making one endless speech."[29] Paul Charles Harris, writing about the play some fourteen years after Miss Phelan's review agreed that "Instead of seeing thought in action, one is burdened with long, tiresome and undramatic speeches obscuring an already muddled plot."[30]

All too often in *The Rugged Path,* Sherwood mounts the sort of soapbox which was a very familiar prop among the proletarian writers of the 1930's. He is distinctly out of character, though by no means insincere, when he takes the stands that Clifford Odets and Albert Maltz and Albert Bein had taken a decade earlier. When Morey tells what he felt on seeing the light burning at the main entrance to the White House upon his return from England, he says, "I thought, 'There is the last light that is left shining anywhere on earth.' I guess I was unduly emotional. But I had the thought that the fuel that kept that light burning was the living spirit of a hundred and thirty million people who were strong and weak, rich and poor, wise and ignorant, black and white, Christian and Jew" (341). This speech might have come directly from such a play as *Let Freedom Ring,* in which case, of course, the light would more likely have been burning outside a union hall than outside the White House.

It is doubtful that a play so ideologically diffuse as *The Rugged Path* could ever have been an artistic success. Possibly as two plays the result would have been somewhat more rewarding. As Sherwood had originally planned, the first play would have been set in America and would have concentrated on some area of American life, similar to that seen in the first act of *The Rugged Path.* Someone like the individualistic journalist, Morey Vinion, would have been spokesman in this play. The second play was to have been set in some occupied country, and the hero was to have been a United States service man. The fusion, partly the result of Sherwood's having gone late in the war on a government mission to the Philippines and other outposts in the Pacific, was unfortunate.

Whereas Sherwood was traditionally a fast, sure writer who produced a play in a matter of weeks and with very little revision and rewriting had it staged, he worked long on the production of *The Rugged Path*; and, once it had been written, its history was one of revision, reversioning, and general alteration. The play was at times abandoned, only to be brought back to life by the author and the Playwrights' Producing Company which finally staged the Broadway production. Spencer Tracy was a natural for the role of Morey Vinion, but he began to lose faith in the play which had at first excited him greatly. In Boston he withdrew from the company, only to be persuaded to return in a matter of hours. But after a run of ten weeks and a total of eighty-one performances on Broadway, the Playwrights' Producing Company had no course but to withdraw the play. Extensive rewriting only served to weaken further the play's already uncertain structure. The inclusion in the middle of the second act of the reception of the news of Morey's probable death by his wife and brother-in-law was a clumsy attempt to create unity between the first and second acts.

Nearly twenty years before *The Rugged Path* was produced Sherwood had written in the preface to *The Queen's Husband*, "Hokum, as the term is applied in these disillusioned states, is the life-blood of the theatre, its animating force, the cause of and the reason for its existence. The theatre is and always has been a nursery of the arts, a romping-ground for man's more childish emotions."[31] These words might have come back to haunt Sherwood after *The Rugged Path*, because from this play the hokum has been excluded, utterly banished, to be replaced by philosophical diatribe. The comic appeal is gone, the sentiment is stale. And Robert Sherwood, now much involved in reducing forty filing cabinets of Harry Hopkins' papers into a single historical volume, *Roosevelt and Hopkins*, is understandably to become less concerned with the fortunes of his sinking play than with his momentous and singularly important history of one phase of World War II.

V The Virtuous Knight

That Robert Sherwood was not effective as a novelist is clearly evident to one who has read *The Virtuous Knight*. Published in 1931, the novel was to receive scant notice, and those few critics who did review it considered it a very feeble attempt on Sherwood's part at writing a historical novel. No reviewer was to give attention to the fact that the book was considerably more than a historical novel with a satirical edge. However, it is quite apparent that Sherwood, whether he intended it or not, was writing an *Entwicklungsroman*. It is for this reason that the book is included in this chapter which deals primarily with the individual reactions of men to war.

In any consideration of Sherwood's literary and philosophical development, *The Virtuous Knight* cannot be ignored. In this book one finds Sherwood experimenting rather fully with themes which are later to emerge in his plays, or which, in some cases, have already been used in his earlier plays. He is also experimenting with techniques of characterization, and much that is later to appear full-blown in *Abe Lincoln in Illinois* is found in the novel, usually in a rudimentary stage of development.

If one can pinpoint a single major flaw in *The Virtuous Knight*, it is its lack of solid form. The plot is allowed to meander, and the result is that much of the emphasis is wrongly placed in Italy, where Martin, the protagonist, is sentenced to death, rather than in the Holy Lands to which he ultimately escapes through the good offices of Boltomy, the captain of the *Apollyon*. By the time Martin gets to the East, the reader has passed the major climax in the book in terms of action. Therefore, if *The Virtuous Knight* is to be read as a historical novel, it must be considered the most dismal of failures. However, the moral and intellectual climax is still to come, so that read as an *Entwicklungsroman,* the book is somewhat easier to justify.

It is clear that Sherwood uses the Third Crusade as background for a story which is primarily concerned with the development of a young man from his earliest years until the time he finally realizes what he believes and what he stands for in life. Martin, Earl of Elcester, represents Sherwood's attempt to produce a Jean Barois or a Jean Christophe or a Eugene Gant.

The attempt is largely unsuccessful. However, this is the justification for Sherwood's spending considerable time on such scenes as Martin's going to London for Richard's coronation; or his unhappy courtship of Melise, daughter of Ralph of Tenber; or his antics in Italy; or his trip aboard the *Apollyon*, during which he had long conversations with Boltomy and met his first Jew; or his capture and virtual adoption by the pagan enemy; or his escape, along with Zarka, from the pagans. Through all of these events, the emphasis is upon Martin's striving toward self-realization. Martin struggles to find a set of values, becomes disillusioned with his king, questions the validity of the Christian claim to the Holy Lands, ingratiates himself among the pagans, comes to see and share their way of life, and makes his ultimate decision to return to his home and his responsibilities; but it is only after he has savored a wide variety of experience that he can reasonably reach such a decision.

The conflict in *The Virtuous Knight* is largely one between Martin, who is unbelievably good most of the time, and society, which is quite believably bad—or at least immoral—all of the time. All sorts of forces are at work to corrupt the exemplar of Christian knighthood: wicked companions, a lecherous valet, a corrupt and irresponsible king, and an enemy which is characterized by the harems it maintains—all these forces combine to make Martin's virtue seem the more unique and the less credible. But Martin emerges with his eternal salvation presumably assured and his virtue still intact. However, he is not the same believing Christian knight who had originally entered the fray. He clearly states his stand toward the end of the book when he says, "I am not lost. In fact, I am one who has found himself by discovering the hollowness of all faith, Christian and Moslem alike"* (361). Sherwood here suggests that Martin has risen above his early parochialism; and this parochialism is suggestive of the narrow patriotism which Sherwood criticizes in many of his plays.

Martin was actively trained in virtue almost from the time he was first able to comprehend. His mentor, Gervas, was a saintly old man who never smiled. When Martin's father lay mortally wounded, he charged Gervas with the responsibility of teaching

*All references are to the first edition of the play (New York: Charles Scribner's Sons, 1931).

Martin to be brave and good and chivalrous and to lead a good life. When Martin was taken to the estate of his maternal grandfather after his father's death, Gervas remained with him and was his teacher until Martin inherited his grandfather's vast properties and left for the Crusades at the head of his own legion.

During his early years, Martin had no companion save the coarse Hugh, son of Shawel, the illiterate chief huntsman of his grandfather's estate. Hugh was stronger by far than Martin, and much less sensitive. As he grew older, Hugh was a happy lecher, pursuing his pleasures in the forests around Elcester. To the sheltered Martin, Hugh's conduct was at once disgraceful and intriguing. Finally, over Gervas' protestations, Martin chose Hugh to be his body servant. "Old Gervas . . . felt that Hugh would be a bad influence. That, however, was just what Martin wanted, although this fact was not known, even to himself" (50). Hugh represented the necessary counterbalance to a life in which Martin ". . . came to understand that everything he did was part of his education. There was no time for anything else. If he rode over into the great forest beyond Ensdown for a stag hunt, it was made plain to him that he did so only because this form of activity helped to train him for the more serious battle of life. . . . The incessant performance of his duty—that, he was assured, was the only right life" (35).

Martin did not live in a society in which duty occupied so important a part in the lives of notables about him as it did in his own. His king, Richard the Lion-Hearted, as is seen in the novel, did not rush into the field of battle in the Holy Lands until he had spent many months enjoying the fleshly pleasures of Messina. The reader is told that "His Grace of Canterbury, whose name was Baldwin, was a robust old scoundrel who had attained his eminence because he could out-talk and out-fight his adversaries. He was not in any sense of the word a holy man, but he was an excellent bishop and one who did much to promote the church as a vigorous, militant factor in the English state. He feared no one, not even God" (77). Episcopal duty never prevented Baldwin from doing what was best for him and the factions he supported.

Upon his grandfather's death, the dutiful Martin was commanded by the king to pay court to Melise, daughter of Ralph of Tenber; he proceeded at once upon this course which could lead only to a marriage which he loathed to think about. This arranged marriage is reminiscent of that which was to take place between the Princess Anne and Prince William of Greck in *The Queen's Husband*. In *The Virtuous Knight,* the reaction is shown from the point of view of the proposed husband, but in *The Queen's Husband* it is shown 'from that of the female. However, in both cases the women involved were in love with other men and ultimately married them. In Martin's case, Melise's running away is the greatest blessing he can hope for because it makes him appear to be the injured party—it is not generally known how reluctant he is to marry—and he can now demonstrate his magnanimity by graciously forgiving the woman who has besmirched his honor. And he can be sure that no one, not even the king, will attempt to arrange a marriage for him soon again. Indeed, the death of the king and the ascent to the throne of his heir, Richard I, followed almost at once by the undertaking by Richard of the Third Crusade, is to involve Martin and all the British nobility in such activity that no further thought is given to his marrying.

Part of Martin's education, indeed a somewhat seamy part, is in the hands of two fellow noblemen who are part of the huge procession following Richard to London for the coronation. Josserant de Buon, represented as being about Martin's age, and Roger of Thursham, a man of about fifty, are much more worldly than Martin. He falls into conversation with them and is to meet with them again as the Crusade proceeds. These two are always portrayed as being carefree and irresponsible; they are more interested in pursuing women than in pursuing the Holy Grail. Martin's reaction to them is very much like his reaction to Hugh: He is shocked but fascinated. He is accepted as a friend by these two noblemen, even though in comparison he is painfully naïve and unworldly. It is Josserant who is to lead to Martin's being sentenced to death in Messina, and it is also Josserant and Roger who, with Hugh's help and the king's tacit sanction, rescue Martin just before his execution is to take place.

Actually the sequence of events at Messina represents the most significant climax in the book; yet it occurs before the story is half over. Martin has been billeted temporarily with Joachim, a cleric of advanced years, who lives in a beautiful villa outside the city. Joachim has a very lovely young housekeeper to whom both Martin and Josserant are drawn. As it turns out, the housekeeper has already been claimed by Joachim; however, she is attracted by Martin's youth and vigor, and suggests that he steal into her room on a given evening. The story is a very old one and, were it less contrived, would read like something from the *Decameron* or *The Canterbury Tales*.

Ironically, Martin, still painfully virtuous, almost yields; but he finally goes out for a walk instead. During the walk, he is pursued by hoodlums bent on robbing him. He flees along the waterfront, hides near a ship, and there meets Boltomy who urges him to take passage and leave the following day for the Holy Lands. Back at the villa, Josserant has stolen into the housekeeper's room and has had his pleasure, being mistaken by the housekeeper for Martin. On leaving, however, he runs into Joachim, who also mistakes him for Martin. Hence, when Martin returns, he is received by the ranting Joachim who turns him over to the authorities and insists upon his death. Richard accedes to Joachim's insistent wish, and Martin is to be executed the following day. When he is rescued, however, Boltomy's ship is waiting to whisk him off.

Obviously, Sherwood's plot is so contrived and so tired that one cannot read it with any enthusiasm. Its every turn is predictable. Further, each turn is achieved not through any notable structural development, but through the author's omniscient relating of events. It is further apparent that Sherwood grew very tired of what he was doing long before he had finished his novel. It is probably a reasonable assumption that his story might better have been told had he pursued more vigorously the rewriting of his unproduced play *Marching as to War* which was about a conscientious objector who refused to go on the Third Crusade with Richard the Lion-Hearted. Martin, rather than being a conscientious objector, is a dupe whose whole life is circumstantially determined.

It must be said of Martin's virtue that the extreme depiction of goodness is consistent with much medieval chivalric writing, and Sherwood was undoubtedly trying to achieve this effect in *The Virtuous Knight*. However, he undermines this effort most severely by superimposing upon the story his own observations regarding war. He says, for example, that "Men were no longer fighting for ideals but for existence, and a bare, meagre existence it was" (251). He then repeats a sentiment which he himself had felt as a war casualty in 1918 and which he had already given voice to in *Waterloo Bridge*. Martin had been wounded in the siege of Acre. He was burned and his legs were injured. After considerable care, "He could now walk without limping, and the skin on his back was sufficient to permit the wearing of a shirt. He could not yet put on his armor, but this inability failed to depress him. Indeed, he wished to postpone for as long as possible the day when he would again be liable to be called into action" (258). And, indeed, it is not long before Martin reaches the decision to leave the crusade and return to England. It is during this flight to the seaport from which he will embark that he is captured by the pagans and by mere chance Kahtan, the sultan's son, saves him from execution because he had defended Kahtan when he was attacked on the way to his dominion.

Sherwood takes his protagonist much more seriously than the average reader has been able to. This is a significant flaw in characterization which was to be overcome most effectively by the time the author wrote *Abe Lincoln in Illinois* and *There Shall Be No Night*. In *The Rugged Path,* the characterization of Morey Vinion again suggests the sort of protagonist which one encounters in Martin; however, Morey is a much more convincing figure than Martin, largely because he is set in a modern context. He is a round figure, whereas the medieval heroic type was essentially flat and often stock. It is when Sherwood tried to make something other than a stock figure of Martin, that his protagonist became unconvincing.

Martin's virtue would have been much easier to believe had he been subjected to real temptation. However, as the character is developed, one has the feeling that what would have been a temptation to the average man was not one to Martin. Even when Martin is on the brink of seducing Zarka, only to turn from her, one has the inescapable feeling that he is trying to prove something to himself and that he approaches the seduction dutifully and without lust. He is more pleased than disappointed when Zarka makes it possible for him to turn from her without having accomplished his mission. If Martin overcomes real temptation at any time in the book, this fact is unrevealed, although, of course, it is sometimes suggested.

Martin's education follows an interesting course, and Sherwood would have the reader believe that the product is a liberal man. Old Gervas was Martin's first and his only formal teacher. However, the most important part of Martin's early education came from Shawel, the huntsman, who first taught Martin how to hunt rabbits. Martin won his first rabbit, only to be made ill by the horror of the victory. Shawel represents the uncouth hunter, the Anglo-Saxon still living in a relatively uncivilized part of the world—an area as yet devoid of the sort of culture which for centuries has characterized the East. This dichotomy is made evident in the lines which read "He [Martin] was glad that he had been captured. The writing in the yet unfolded Roll of Fate was changing before his eyes, from the cold, rugged, upright Gothic of old Gervas's Bible to the soft, graceful, gently rhythmical Arabic of the *Rubáiyát*" (274).

Martin's first introduction to the heretical thought which he is later to find so appealing comes from the forthright captain, Boltomy. Also on Boltomy's ship is the rabbi of Naim, Machir ben Azariah. When he and Martin talk at length, Martin is amazed by the wisdom and insight of this old man who says to him, " 'Thou shalt have no other gods before me.' To you young men of young races those are not more than words taught to you by priests. You were not born knowing them, as we were. You were born with tribal memories of paganism, and when you look upon such glories of antiquity as this image of Aphrodite, those memories are awakened, and you forget that you have been baptized in the holy waters of an alien faith. . . . I often wonder . . . whether the ultimate effect of these Crusades won't be far different from that which was hoped for and anticipated by the pontiffs who have instigated them" (205). But Martin, still the believer, is also somewhat shocked by what the venerable rabbi has said. This speech by the rabbi, of course, represents the denouement of the story. It is regrettable structurally that the denouement comes so long before the ultimate unfolding of the events which are to give it point.

Also instrumental in teaching Martin is Cimon, the Greek mercenary who is to die by being shot from a Christian cannon against the walls of Acre. Cimon represents the rationalist who is engaged in a religious conflict only because soldiering—actually military engineering—is his profession. He serves for a time on one side, then on the other. He views both sides dispassionately, and, indeed, cannot even become personally involved in the events which lead to his own death. As his body catapults through the air toward the walls of the pagan stronghold, he laughs wildly; but Sherwood makes a point of saying that he is amused, not hysterical. Cimon is in many ways comparable to Achilles Weber in *Idiot's Delight*. He has no loyalty to either side; but, unlike Weber, Cimon has loyalties which are above and beyond such conflicts as the present one. Cimon is a cultivated man who introduces Martin to the *Rubáiyát*. He lives the whole of his life as though believing that all of life is, as Oscar Wilde says, a speculation rather than a sacrament.

Kahtan and the sultan are also instrumental in Martin's education. Kahtan is avaricious, in some ways a pagan counterpart of what Martin might have been had he remained in Britian. He needs the stimulation of conflict in order that life be meaningful. The sultan, on the other hand, is a mellow and peaceful person who keeps a cheetah chained in a corner of his lavish apartment. Fish play in a pool just beyond the reach of the chained beast who occasionally surges forth to catch a fish, only to be rudely reminded of his captivity by the sudden pull on his neck when he reaches the end of his tether. This beast, of course, is an allegorical representation of the surging forces within men; in medieval terms the beast represents the body and the chain the soul. This symbol is reinforced by Kahtan and the sultan, for Kahtan represents physical conquest whereas his father represents the reason which comes with age.

The legend of Pheros is told Martin by Boltomy as they reach Pheros on their way to the Holy Lands. Briefly, this is the story of the young girl, Callirhoe of Cythera, who was to be married to Thalos. However, Alexander commanded that a statue of Callirhoe be created by Praxiteles in the finest Parian marble. Until Callirhoe was brought to Alexander and the statute of her was made by Praxiteles, the young girl was to remain a virgin. On the trip to Alexander's stronghold in the area where Persia and Syria meet, the ship carrying the beautiful girl, the venerable sculptor, and the fine piece of Parian marble foundered off Pheros and all aboard were lost. There was great mourning, and Thalos came to Pheros where he intended to throw himself into the sea which had claimed his betrothed. However, as he approached the headlands, he walked into a grove of cypresses and there he beheld his beloved, lifelike, but immortalized in marble.

It is to Pheros that Martin and Zarka make their ways when they escape from the sultan. The novel closes here, and Sherwood intended to tie the legend in with the ending. However, the connection is never fully realized and the ending is such that one might wish Martin had remained with the sultan and married his daughter, Nafisah, so that the sultan's vision might have been realized, as he expressed it: "I believed that the son born to you and my daughter would be the perfect fulfillment, the truly civilized man in whom were assembled the elements of all men, Christian and Moslem, occidental and oriental, white and brown, not to conflict with each other, but to blend in a supernal harmony" (391).

The reviewer for *Outlook* was correct in his conclusion that ". . . the book falls between two stools and is neither very good historical romance—the satirist never being concerned to discover or convey the atmosphere of the period of which he writes —nor very good satire, since it is too slow moving and tenuous as a novel."[32] This reviewer does feel that "the theme is cleverly handled, the style [is] easy and agreeable, and the historical detail and description are good." It must be remembered, of course, that *Outlook's* reviewer, like all the others, was suggesting that the book was a failure as one of two possible types: historical romance and satire. He did not allow the possibility that Sherwood might have been essentially concerned with writing neither of these types of novel. F. T. Marsh, writing in the New York *Times,* calls the book over-long and amorphous. He accuses the author of having ". . . either muffled or deliberately cast aside every dramatic possibility,"[33] and in this comment Marsh has focused his attention upon the book's real failure.

Sherwood was not temperamentally suited to the writing of novels. The theater gave him the immediate rewards and satisfactions to which he best responded. It was not entirely the failure of *The Virtuous Knight* which turned him from the writing of novels; rather, it was his blood tie with theater. *The Virtuous Knight* remains an isolated but revealing phenomenon in the body of Sherwood's published work.

CHAPTER 5

Sceptres Uneasily Held

"We've expelled the Hapsburgs from Austria, but not . . . from ourselves."
— Reunion in Vienna

FROM THE TIME that he wrote *The Road to Rome* in 1926 until he wrote *Reunion in Vienna* in 1931, Robert Sherwood was groping for a satisfactory means of saying what was in his mind. His attempts in *The Love Nest, The Queen's Husband, Waterloo Bridge, This Is New York*, and *The Virtuous Knight* were abortive. However, each of these works brought him a step closer to what he was finally to achieve in the plays which begin with *The Petrified Forest* and end with *There Shall Be No Night. Reunion in Vienna* stands chronologically between his notable failures and his most significant successes. This high comedy in the Continental tradition was in itself a notable success, as will be seen. In the play Sherwood gained the mastery of technique he had been trying to achieve, and he achieved it without bringing to the drama the serious philosophical messages for which his later plays were to be vehicles.

The failure of Sherwood's works which fell between *The Road to Rome* and *Reunion in Vienna* is due largely to his attempts to be essentially philosophical and serious most of the time, relieving the seriousness only occasionally with often untimely bursts of broad humor. But in *Reunion in Vienna* the philosophical level is underplayed, and the broad humor is replaced with sophisticated wit. Philosophically, the play carries less weight than *The Road to Rome*. However, in terms of urbane humor, *Reunion in Vienna* surpasses anything that Sherwood has written.

The Queen's Husband and *Reunion in Vienna* are discussed in this chapter because the two plays bear broad similarities to each other. They are not basically similar in theme; however, each is concerned with the place of royalty in an age when constitutional government is becoming universal. More than any of Sherwood's other plays following *The Road to Rome*, *The Queen's Husband* represents a step, however faltering, in the direction of *Reunion in Vienna*.

Both of these plays are largely escapist in nature. Sherwood acknowledges this characteristic in regard to *Reunion in Vienna*, the preface of which begins, "This play is another demonstration of the escape mechanism in operation." Willard Thorp suggests that by this time in Sherwood's career, ". . . he had lost hope in rational solutions. Hypertrophied rationalism was now the enemy."[1] This statement applies, however, to *The Queen's Husband* as well to *Reunion in Vienna*. In the earlier play the rational solutions come largely from emotional causes; but the solutions, when analyzed, are more emotional than rational. In *Reunion in Vienna* sentiment runs wild and is encouraged—albeit for the purpose ultimately of killing it completely—by the representative of reason in the play, the psychiatrist, Dr. Anton Krug.

In both of these plays, Sherwood is seeking answers to generalized problems. *The Queen's Husband* treats the question of what power and meaning monarchy can have in the contemporary world; but, more broadly, it deals also with the basic question of human rights. *Reunion in Vienna* represents the retreats that men make into the past in order to blind themselves to the rapid changes which their society foists upon them. Whereas the earlier play became at times a sort of philosophical talkathon, the later play moved at a pleasing, sprightly pace.

Alfred Lunt and Lynn Fontanne were cast in the lead roles in *Reunion in Vienna*. Even as one reads through the play thirty-odd years after its first performance, it is difficult to dissociate the theater's first couple from the roles which they so magnificently played during the Broadway run. Their respective parts seem to have been written specifically for them. It is completely possible that Sherwood had them in mind when he wrote the play, and that this is what made *Reunion in Vienna* so much better than his immediately preceding works. It must be noted that

Lunt and Fontanne were among Sherwood's closest friends and that he came to depend very much upon their critical judgments in the production of his later plays. It does not seem extravagant to speculate that much of the light humorous spirit which was to alleviate the philosophical solemnity of his later plays is a benefaction derived from these two great theatrical spirits. But this is only speculation and, like all speculation, it might be completely incorrect. It is clear, however, that by the time Sherwood wrote *Reunion in Vienna,* something had happened to change his basic attitude toward what he was doing. He was only a year removed from the writing of *Waterloo Bridge, This Is New York,* and *The Virtuous Knight;* yet in this year he had learned fluency and he had come to moderate the introspection which, in his last four or five works, had weakened the dramatic effectiveness of what he was writing. *Reunion in Vienna* was the beginning of Sherwood's "golden decade."

I The Queen's Husband

Marie, queen of Rumania from 1914 until 1927, made a state visit to the United States in 1926. The daily presses carried considerable information about the visit of this reigning monarch and presented readers with a great deal of detailed background material about the queen. From the facts which emerged, it was easy to surmise that Marie was a forceful ruler; it was also clear that she was a woman of considerable talent and ingenuity. She had written several books, and she had distinguished herself for her courage in working with the Red Cross to alleviate the suffering of her people after Rumania's surrender to Germany in 1917.

Marie's consort, Ferdinand, was somewhat eclipsed by his wife's prominence. He was much less involved in affairs of state than she, and it was not difficult to imagine that Marie played the role of absolute dictator in the family situation, even though she was constitutionally prevented from doing so in the national situation. Ferdinand was honored by his people, and after the war was to return to Bucharest in triumph. After he was crowned king of Greater Rumania in 1922, he enacted reforms, but he was beset by political and domestic problems which indirectly led to his death in 1927. During Marie's visit to the United

States, the American public, through what the newspapers reported, came to look upon Ferdinand as a pawn. It is in this way that Robert Sherwood was to present him in the person of King Eric VIII, ruler of ". . . a mythical and anonymous kingdom, situated on an island in the North Sea, somewhere between Denmark and Scotland"* (7). Queen Marie is presented in the person of Queen Martha who, in the course of the action, goes to the United States on an official visit aimed at winning American aid for her heroic little kingdom. Martha rules her people, with the help of General Northrup and Lord Birten, by steamroller tactics while her dispirited husband plays checkers with Phipps, his loyal footman.

Sherwood's title, of course, implies the situation which Eric VIII is in. While he is not coldly indifferent to his people, he is, on the one hand, too henpecked to offer much resistance to his wife's dictations; on the other, he is too much in the thrall of General Northrup to protect the people from the brand of military totalitarianism which Northrup has imposed upon them. Before the play has been long in progress, the audience is aware that Eric is powerless to act directly in behalf of his subjects. One's first impression of him is that he is befuddled, resigned, and not very bright. The first clue to the king's real personality and, incidentally, to his method of coping with the impossible—usually represented by his wife—comes when Queen Martha, at General Northrup's behest, directs her husband to sign official orders for the execution of a large number of people whom Northrup has arrested as dangerous to the state. The king has had these documents for some time, but he has not signed them because he does not wish the executions to take place. He realizes the futility of arguing with Northrup and the queen, but he also realizes that the executions cannot be carried out without his signed orders. When the queen presses him to sign the documents, he cannot find them on his desk and he orders his private secretary, Freddy Granton, to search for them. Finally Freddy finds them and brings them to the king. By this time the queen and Northrup have left, and the king tells Freddy, ". . . take them out and lose them again" (55).

A further clue to the king's personality is given in the course of

*All references are to the first edition of the play (New York: Charles Scribner's Sons, 1928).

his game of checkers with Phipps. The king is not a very good player and appears to have a rather bad memory; however, it is soon evident that he is really quite cagey and is completely capable of winning when it suits his purposes to do so. In a sense, the king's checker games parallel the contrived, calculated games which he plays with those who are usurping his power. He lets them appear to be winning, Sherwood seems to imply, but he saves his master stroke until it is needed and can be used most effectively.

The national crisis which occurs during the course of the play is explained by Sherwood in his stage directions before the first speech is given. He describes the people of Eric's kingdom as being ". . . occupied principally with shipping, fishing, and agriculture. The limited nature of the industrial activity, together with excessive overpopulation, have resulted in a dangerous unemployment problem and consequent discontent in the laboring classes—all of which indicates a revolution in Act II" (7). The unique feature of this play is that the revolution is presented sympathetically, but is always viewed through the windows of the palace which is under attack by the revolutionaries. One never really comes into contact with the workers at all; even their representatives, Dr. Fellman and Laker, are seen but little. Sympathy for the masses is engendered almost solely through the emphasis on the totalitarianism shown by General Northrup throughout the play. The king, of course, sides with the masses, and would be glad indeed to be relieved of the constricting responsibility of his kingship. Princess Anne states in so many words that "Father would like to be free himself" (17).

The Princess Anne is frequently in dispute with her mother. She turns to her father for what little support he can give her against the dictatorial queen. She loves her father, but finds it difficult to respect him. She has never really been able to depend upon him because her mother has always undercut his decisions and he has failed to protest. Anne, who is in love with Freddy Granton, hopes that by some miracle she might eventually be able to marry him. But Freddy is not a logical mate for the princess; his father is in trade! And to make it all the worse, the trade is plumbing, albeit the elder Granton is a wealthy plumbing supply wholesaler who is one of the principal contributors to Northrup's campaign fund.

A crisis occurs in Anne's romance with Freddy when, during the first act, Lord Birten announces that arrangements have been concluded for Princess Anne to make a highly advantageous marriage with Prince William of Greck. He also graciously praises the queen for her efforts in bringing the engagement about. Then he tells the horrified Anne the terms of the marriage: ". . . the marriage announcement provides that the Princess Anne will, of course, become Empress of Greck, in due time. Her eldest son will be the heir to the throne, and her second son will become the Crown Prince in our own dear land. Thus, in the future, two brothers will be reigning at the same . . ." (34-35). But Anne interrupts him and blurts out, "Two brothers—my sons! So the contract provides that I shall produce two male children. Well—how do you know I can?" The queen cautions her daughter that she is being indelicate, and the aroused Anne replies passionately, "That's just what it is— indelicate, horrible, revolting! It's awful enough to be married off to some rotten degenerate—but to be treated as though I were a brood mare turned out in a stud farm—oh, God!" (35). It is just this sort of outburst which Sherwood learns to control by the time he writes *Reunion in Vienna*. The effect here, while comic, is too broad and unrestrained to be artistically sound.

Viewing the situation purely from the standpoint of plot, Sherwood is obviously using the arranged marriage to show the disadvantages of monarchy even to those who are to reign under it. Anne is enough her mother's daughter to be a determined young woman; but she is also enough her father's daughter to loathe the thought of having to rule. The king, who in his silence and withdrawal understands his daughter remarkably well, ruminates in the last act of the play, "Poor Anne! She'll be a rotten queen" (153). And in this statement he sums up Sherwood's attitude toward inherited eminence.

The fundamental conflict in the play is the conflict between Anne and the forces which would tell her whom to marry. The conflict is much concerned with human freedom of choice. But the broader conflict, which is here used mostly as a back-ground for the drama, is one of much more moment: it concerns freedom of choice for the subjects in this mythical and anonymous kingdom. These people have been deprived of the right of free elections, and they have been forced into a life of economic oppression. As Anne's unhappiness at her arranged marriage increases, the uneasiness of the citizens at their oppression runs parallel in development. And as the unhappy event which will unite Prince William of Greck and Princess Anne is to take place in the cathedral, the revolutionary forces are prepared to show their ultimate defiance by exploding bombs in the holy edifice. But in the end, as in a fairy tale of old, happiness is to prevail; the king is to assert himself and in one memorable day is to marry his daughter to the man she really loves—the king himself performs the hasty ceremony—and send them off on a ship bound for Panama. King Eric is also to dissolve Parliament, thereby clearing the way for free popular elections.

It is ironic—but not unusual—that as monarchies weaken, the monarchs come increasingly to take a democratic stand; but those anti-liberals who arise, often in military ranks, at such a time become totalitarian as General Northrup is represented as being in this play. But by far the greatest irony of the play is found in the fact that Queen Martha, for all her officious direction of events within her kingdom, is revealed to be the unwitting pawn of the forces which would destroy her and her way of life, whereas the quiet and seemingly ineffectual Eric saves his subjects from the horrors of a revolution and offers to them the rights for which they have been willing to fight to the death. Martha suffers from a confused patriotism, a misplaced loyalty; but Eric, who at the end of the play is far more analytical in his thinking than Martha, does not lose sight of the fact that his basic loyalty must be to his people and, in a narrower sense, to his daughter.

It cannot validly be said that there is any specific anti-war sentiment in *The Queen's Husband.* King Eric does prevent a revolution, but his doing so is because of his concern with human rights, not with the sort of out-and-out pacifism which appears in *The Road to Rome* or later in *Idiot's Delight.* There are no pacifist diatribes in the play; but there are political diatribes against the sort of government which Northrup has imposed upon the people.

The second act of *The Queen's Husband* becomes rather exciting. The queen has departed for the United States. Just before her departure she has told Eric that ". . . I shall come back with the money that we need—even if I have to go straight to the President of the United States himself" (61). The king replies, "God help the President of the United States" (62). This remark makes a natural ending for Act I. The second act, which occurs two months later, opens with King Eric and Phipps engaged, as always, in a game of checkers. The game is being pursued stoically even though a revolution is about to break out and the palace is filled with soldiers.

It is soon announced by Freddie Granton that Lord Birten has offered a resolution in Parliament calling for the proclamation of Northrup as dictator with absolute power. This event, of course, creates not only an obvious pretext for the Liberals to begin the revolution, but it also presents a direct challenge to the king's authority. However, he cannot move rapidly for he knows that Northrup has the army mobilized and that the fleet is in position to bombard the city. The king expresses no personal concern, but he is very much perplexed because he realizes that his people are in very great danger and that Northrup will ". . . butcher them" (72). When Anne suggests that she and Freddie might get away in the confusion of the revolution, the king dismisses this idea saying, "There's too much disturbance as it is" (73). The king tells Anne, "Thank God your mother isn't here now. She'd be more ruthless than Northrup himself."

The first skirmishes of revolution begin, but there is no formal declaration that a revolution exists. The palace is soon to be attacked. Northrup has threatened from his safe position in the War Office that naval guns will begin shelling if the revolutionists do not surrender. It is the realization that these naval guns "could destroy half the city in a few minutes" (78) that really brings about the turning point in the king's involvement in the disturbance. Fellman comes to see him, actually to demand his abdication. He tells the king that a large number of the people are devoted to him, but that a new deal is needed. At that point, the naval guns open fire, and Fellman declares, "Now the murder will start" (109). The king can endure Northrup's dictation no longer, and he calls the admiralty and orders an armistice.

The king, who has not acted in years, now acts in such a way as to bring down upon his head the curses of all the anti-liberal forces which General Northrup represents. Before King Eric gives his order for an armistice, General Northrup has challenged him severely by saying, ". . . I'm running this show and I intend to run it in my own way" (94). But the king is not to permit him to do so without a fight, and his resentment mounts very noticeably as he says to Northrup, "You have bullied your way into the dictatorship, thereby making me more of a cipher than ever. Your next step, obviously, is the presidency." Northrup resents this insinuation, and acts especially resentful that the king—quite correctly—has really classed Northrup with those very anarchists from whom he is supposedly defending the kingdom. He tells the king: "The crown will remain supreme, inviolate, as long as God spares me to fight in Your Majesty's defense." But then Northrup tells him that the crown is ". . . a symbol—an emblem—and the people of this country are so ignorant, so backward, that they must have symbols" (95).

After the order for the armistice has been given, Northrup tells the king that this is the last order that he will ever give, and the real power struggle begins. Superimposed upon the struggle is the impending marriage of the Princess Anne, which is to take place in a week in the presence of much of the royalty of Europe. When Eric reminds Northrup that he is king "by the grace of God," Northrup says to him: "The grace of God! Don't use that catch-phrase on me! It's all very well to impress the public with it—but you know, and I know, that you're the King by the grace of me, and my army—and you'll be King only as long as I and my army are on hand to keep you on the throne" (115).

The king, however, now becomes the modern monarch and tells Northrup that his power is with the people and that they, not Northrup, will keep him on the throne. Northrup asks, "Are you referring to the loyal subjects who have just been shelling your palace?" The king replies: "I am referring to those backward, ignorant fools who are impressed by catch phrases and symbols" (119). The king's faith here is, in a much longer speech, repeated by Harry Van in *Idiot's Delight* when he tells the doctor that the gullibility of mankind has given him faith. "It has made me sure that no matter how much the meek may be bulldozed or gypped they *will* eventually inherit the earth."

The act ends with news that an assassin has made an unsuccessful attempt on the life of General Northrup. The crowd outside the palace is at a high pitch of excitement. When the king is told that the mob is violently hostile, he decides that he must go out upon his balcony and calm the people. Granton and Anne are worried lest he be in danger of assassination; but the king says in the closing speech of the act: "Don't worry, Anne, I'll be perfectly safe. If the revolutionists couldn't hit Northrup at close range, they won't harm me" (123). He goes onto the balcony and the curtain falls as the mob outside bursts into cheering which "swells into a gigantic roar."

The final act takes place a week later. The queen has returned, the palace has been repaired, and the princess is this day to be married to Prince William. The queen is very busy: She is dressing, directing, and composing prayers for the archbishop to read. She enjoys all of this immensely, and she especially enjoys complaining about how much of the responsibility has fallen to her. The king, having had his moment of glory, gives every appearance now of having settled back into his ineffectual role, and it is not until the end of the act that one has cause to believe otherwise. The queen inspects her husband and asks him where his Order of St. Christopher is. He tells her he didn't have room for it, and she tells him, "Well, *find* room for it!" to which he can only reply with a feeble, "I shall, dear" (130).

Sherwood succeeds quite well in capturing all of the hypocrisy of an arranged royal wedding. Everyone is to smile and give the appearance of ecstatic happiness. Yet during this act Prince William comes to talk with Princess Anne and begins his interview with her by saying, "I may as well begin by telling you I don't like you. I don't like you a bit" (137). Anne offers to release William, but he assures her that this will not do. Rather he tells her, "I am anxious to say a few things while our relationship is still on a fairly friendly basis. . . . I came here to ask you to be a reasonably good sport" (138). As the interview progresses, Anne becomes more and more upset; and, when Freddie accidentally stumbles into the room, she falls into his arms and it is quite apparent to William that the two are lovers. He promptly tells the queen what the king has already known for some time. Freddie is arrested, and it is first decided that he shall be executed and then that he shall be exiled to Panama. In the midst of all of this hubbub, Dr. Fellman and Laker are to arrive, and the king is to try to persuade them that the revolutionaries should desist from any demonstrations during the wedding ceremony. The king fears that the wedding party may all be blown to bits, and at this point, Anne is less disturbed at this thought than at that of marrying Prince William. Obviously, the king at this point has not reached the decision to save his daughter from the impending marriage.

Northrup arrives to report that Freddie has been arrested, and, during his visit, Dr. Fellman and Laker are announced. This precipitates a great commotion, at the end of which the king uses his long forgotten regal authority to dissolve Parliament. Lord Birten reminds the king that in doing so he must remember that now the state ceases to exist, but the king counters dramatically, "Oh, no, it doesn't, Birten. I am the state!" (176). He then appoints Dr. Fellman to the premiership and orders him to form a cabinet at once. His next official act is to have Freddie brought to him, along with Anne; and, acting again under the power of the Constitution which he had read the night before, he marries them. He then adds the words "and wife" to Freddie's deportation order, and sends the two young people on their way. Having done this, he tells Phipps in the last speech in the play, "I will be going to the Cathedral now. But I will be coming back, shortly" (190).

The Queen's Husband had a moderate run of one-hundred-twenty-five performances on Broadway. In comparison to the other plays of the season, this production was considered to be an enjoyable and diverting light comedy. Ronald Young turned in a memorable performance as King Eric VIII. The play received little critical notice, and often the notice it did receive dwelt upon what the play wasn't rather than on what the play was. For example, the critic for *Outlook* stated that the play had nothing offensive or dull about it. It was not in bad taste, and it contained no muddled thinking; nor was there about it the heavy hand of the propagandist. However, this critic had to admit that ". . . the story itself is neither significant nor startlingly original."[2] He also felt that the play was weakened by all of the talk that was necessary in getting the revolution under way. Most critics complained that the play was shallow; some called it pretentious. Actually, Mr. Seldes dealt most fairly with this charge when he wrote in *Dial* that such charges seemed not to be *apropos* in this case because Sherwood's ". . . play is a bagatelle in which he does not seek the secret of life, as he did in *The Road to Rome*."³

The chief weakness which Seldes points out is very noticeable: ". . . the character of the king is not coherent; perhaps it would be better to say that the two characters given to the king do not cohere. . . . we get, as *denouement*, not something astute he has done in advance, but a mere accident by which the revolt ends. The king is neither wise enough nor foolish enough."⁴ It is in Sherwood's treatment of the play's protagonist that he is most often out of control. There is nothing about Eric which would lead one to believe that he could forcefully put into effect any scheme which he thought necessary. The chips have fallen well for him, and he has succeeded in *The Queen's Husband* in two major accomplishments: he has quelled a revolution and brought political determination to his subjects; and he has prevented the marriage of his daughter to a man she loathed, at the same time seeing her married to the man she loved. But the entire play is based upon incredible assumptions, and the presentation is thoroughly romantic. Indeed, there is much about the play which is strongly suggestive of the medieval romance, a literary form in which Sherwood had much interest at this point in his development.

Viewed merely as a bagatelle, *The Queen's Husband* is diverting. The play in some of its speeches represented a step toward greater fluency, but it did not represent a major dramatic or philosophical accomplishment on the part of the author. The action, especially in the third act, is much too diffuse, and the motivation is much too dependent upon fortuitous circumstances for it to be convincing.

II Reunion in Vienna

Viennese comedy was popular on Broadway in 1931. And the most popular of the Viennese comedies of the season was Robert Sherwood's *Reunion in Vienna*, an American impersonation. It had an initial run of 248 performances as opposed to 164 performances for Ladilaus Fodor's *A Church Mouse*, 151 performances for Ferenc Molnar's *The Good Fairy* which starred Helen Hayes, and twenty performances for Chester Erskin's adaptation of Lazlo Fodor's *I Love an Actress*. The play was to reëstablish Sherwood's reputation as playwright at a time when many critics were beginning to wonder whether *The Road to Rome* would ever be surpassed or even equaled by its author. *Reunion in Vienna* endures even today as one of the most lilting, urbane comedies ever produced by an American dramatist.

The play bears a very close affinity to Molnar's *The Guardsman*, although ironically its over-all effect is even more Continental than the effect achieved by Molnar. The Lunts had acted in *The Guardsman*, as had Helen Westley who was to play Frau Lucher in the Sherwood comedy. There can be little doubt that Sherwood had the Lunts in mind when he created Elena Krug and Rudolf Maximilian. It is hard to imagine anyone but the Lunts in these two parts.

Essentially it can be said that *Reunion in Vienna* is a non-philosophical play with an extremely philosophical preface. The gloom of the preface is totally in opposition to the light frivolity of the play itself, and is led into by Sherwood's admission that the play is an escape from reality on his part. He then launches into a presentation of reality as he sees it and ends with the conclusion that "Man may not have time to complete the process of his own doing before the unknown forces have combined to burst the bubble of his universe"* (xvi). But none of the gloom of this preface is transmitted to *Reunion in Vienna*, and the drama does not consider in detail the more profound and serious questions of life.

The scene of the entire action of the play is the Vienna of 1930, and the total time lapse of the action is less than twenty-four hours. The Allied forces which came into Vienna at the conclusion of World War I had deposed the Hapsburgs who were ultimately to be exiled. Vienna is now officially the capital of a republic, and the days of Franz Josef and his line are preserved only in the Baroque palaces which dot the city, in Viennese waltzes, in *Kaffee mit Schlag*, in the Sacher Hotel, and —most importantly—in the hearts of many of the people. When Sherwood visited Vienna in 1928, he immediately felt that he was in the domain of the Hapsburgs, even though there was— officially, at least—not a Hapsburg in the city. His intuition was reaffirmed when he visited Frau Sacher's hotel which still

*All references are to the first edition of the play (New York: Charles Scribner's Sons. 1932).

preserved as much as it could the memories of bygone splendor of those happy days when its guest register for virtually any week read like a *Who's Who* of European nobility.

Sherwood saw Vienna when the nobility was being replaced by the members of the lower and middle classes who had risen to positions of importance in a once strongly and exclusively structured society. The stepping stone to the new society was to be found in the professions, and the representative of the new society in *Reunion in Vienna* is Dr. Anton Krug, a skilled surgeon who, because he opposed the Hapsburgs, was transferred from his position as an army doctor and was set to hard labor in rock quarries where his hands became insensitive and were finally crushed so that surgery was no longer possible for him. As a result, Krug became a psychiatrist when the Hapsburg dynasty finally ended its rule, and it is in this position that the audience comes to know him in the play. Krug, because of his past experiences, should harbor a hatred for the Hapsburgs; but he is a rational man and will not permit himself to hate. The patience which centuries of subservience had taught his family has in Anton become tolerance.

Anton is married to a very beautiful woman, Elena. Now past thirty, she has remained almost as appealing as she was at seventeen when His Serene Highness Rudolf Maximilan took her as his mistress. The excitement of those years has remained in Elena's memory, but she is now the dutiful, faithful, and nearly domesticated wife of a noted psychiatrist and teacher; and she tries not to dwell on the lost past but to live toward the hopeful future which she will share with her husband. She refuses to awaken the ghosts of her most romantic period, and it appears that Elena is essentially very well adjusted. Indeed, both Anton and Elena appear to be so well adjusted that there seems almost to be a lack of spontaneity in their marriage, and this is precisely the impression which Sherwood was working to achieve.

The ghosts which Elena does not permit herself to awaken are awakened for her early in the play. Two of Anton's adoring students are sent into Elena's parlor where Anton hopes they will learn something of social grace from his wife. One of these feckless bumpkins has recently returned from a vacation at Nice, and in the course of her conversation she reveals that she took a taxicab there, whose driver turned out to be the Archduke Rudolf Maximilian. She tells of how he stopped the cab, came into the back seat, and kissed her because she was Viennese. Elena listens to this tale in silence, and then asks "What did he look like?" (34). This simple five-word question is a most skillful stroke on Sherwood's part, for it reveals what the final outcome of the play must be. Ilse's answer is that "He looked as if he'd stepped right out of one of those portraits in the old palace."

Elena's question is very well prepared for. When Anton leaves his wife alone with his two students, he does so in order to have a psychoanalytical session with a woman from Pennsylvania who is suffering from extreme frustration because she cannot cease comparing her husband with her first lover. Anton tells Elena that his advice to this woman is that "She must find her first lover, and have a good look at him as he is now. He's a manufacturer of dental supplies. I think she'll be cured" (29). The psychological generalization which prompts this prescription is clearly a prescription which he would give to any woman who has for ten or fifteen years cherished the memory of an early lover; and generally speaking, the prescription would be a fairly effective one, accomplishing very readily the exact results which the psychiatrist is working toward. But it soon becomes clear that such a prescription, were it given to Elena, would be sure to backfire.

By the time Anton's students meet with Elena, the audience already knows through Anton's father that a clandestine celebration is being planned to commemorate the hundredth anniversary of the birth of Franz Josef. Various members of the deposed nobility have been invited to this arcane gathering which is to be held at the Hotel Lucher. Old Frau Lucher has bribed the police so that the party will not be interrupted and the guests, most of whom are *personæ non gratæ* in Austria, will not be embarrassed. There is even a wild rumor that the Archduke Rudolf Maximilian will attend the celebration, although not many people believe this, for he surely cannot cross the Austrian border without being detected.

No sooner have Anton's students left than Kathie, the Krug's maid, announces that a small delegation led by Frau Lucher is waiting upon Elena. Now Elena, still excited at having received news of Rudolf, is to receive her special invitation to the small and very select gathering which Frau Lucher is arranging. Before she receives the small delegation, old Krug tells Elena what they are here for; and Elena, fearing the temptation which she knows such a reunion would subject her to, tells Anton that she doesn't want to see these people. But Anton, always entirely self-confident, dismisses her objections and apprehensions by saying, "Why not? They're friends of yours, aren't they?" (42). Anton, of course, knows of his wife's past romance with Rudolf; but he views this romance with a sophistication explained more easily by the fact that he is a European than by the fact that he is a psychiatrist, although his professional outlook undoubtedly adds to the *savoir faire* which he manifests throughout the play.

Sherwood has to say little directly to indicate that Elena has remained lovely through the years. On stage during most of the play, she presents living evidence of this fact. However, her enduring loveliness is given emphasis during her interview with Frau Lucher and the Count and Countess von Stainz who have come from London for the celebration. The count rather touchingly says, "Don't mind our gaping at you, Elena. It makes us think that maybe we haven't grown old, either" (47). There is ever the implication that because Elena and Rudolf have escaped the ravages of time, perhaps time can be turned back and happier days can be relived. This is the essence of the sentimental romanticism of the play. But this romanticism is balanced by those parts of the drama which are realistic in their outlook. Anton represents the new Austria, and Elena tries to believe in the new Austria. When the countess bemoans the passing of the Vienna which she had known, Elena tells her that the city's agonies ". . . aren't death agonies . . . They're the throes of childbirth. A new life is being created" (50). She even assures her former friends that "I have forgotten. And my dear old friends, I advise you to forget, too." But the Countess von Stainz answers for Elena as well as for herself when she says, "You're asking a great deal of people who have nothing but memories to live on" (61). The frustration of the woman from Pennsylvania is directly comparable to the frustration which the countess implies in this statement; but the frustration of the Pennsylvanian is much more easily cured than are the sentiment and nostalgia of those who remember Vienna in her greatness.

Elena does not wish to attend Frau Lucher's sentimental reunion; indeed, she fears going to it. She has gained control over her emotions by expunging from her memory all of that sentiment which might disquiet her. She does not wish to risk the equanimity which she has fought for and won over the years. But Anton, more confident of her adjustment than she, urges her to attend. When she is adamant in her refusal, it is revealed to her that Rudolf has left Nice with the intention of being present for the affair. When Anton hears this, he leaves the decision to Elena, and she remains firm in her decision not to go. However, as the first act ends, there is no question that she will attend for she has already yielded to her nostalgia, and this yielding is signaled as the curtain falls with the playing of *The Dollar Princess Waltz* to which she dances with her father-in-law.

Rudolf's entrance in act two is one of the best prepared for and best executed entrances in American theater. Rudolf has already been made legendary in the preceding act. The audience has no doubt that he will arrive and is eagerly awaiting him when he suddenly appears in the room where Frau Lucher is preparing for the evening's festivities. She is unaware of his approach and has no warning of his presence until he ". . . administers a loving whack to her ample bottom" (86) and greets her with, "Good evening, venerable strumpet. Still wearing the red flannel drawers?" whereupon he proceeds to find out. This action is carried over almost directly, incidentally, from *The Guardsman*.

Rudolf is all that a Hapsburg should be. Handsome even in the crude Tyrolean costume which he has had to wear in order to sneak across the border, he is also spirited and proud. As soon as he enters the Hotel Lucher, he takes command and his superciliousness is a delight to all who suffer it, for it is a recreation of an age which has been lost. Rudolf is still archduke: his title may not be officially recognized by the authorities now in power, but one's birthright cannot be legislated away, and Rudolf gives ample proof of this. By his every action Rudolf demonstrates the validity of his statement that Vienna is hopelessly defunct because "They drained the blood from Vienna when they removed us" (91). The sterile, uncultivated, hopelessly bourgeois students who appear briefly in the first act represent those into whose hands the city has fallen. It is very easy to see that these peasants gone professional cannot do anything to vitalize a city which reveled gaily in the insane antics of such as Rudolf. Sanity has now taken over, and the city's spirit has been drained, neutralized, devitalized. And what has happened to Vienna has happened to Elena. The madness has gone from her life and has been replaced by reason; Sherwood is obviously at this point in his career still too much the romantic to accept reason at the expense of vitality.

As soon as Rudolf appears on the stage, one realizes what the outcome of the play must be. But this realization does not cause one's interest to flag; indeed, the audience's appetite is whetted by it. Joseph Wood Krutch made the observation that in *Reunion in Vienna* "The battle is sham because neither [Elena nor Rudolf] has any intention of holding out and the joke is inherent in the fact that the struggle is over nothing except those inessentials invented for the purpose of keeping the game from being either too simple or too soon over."[5] The fact that the decision is obvious makes the playful banter of the drama the more delightful. This is the Continental touch, and indeed it is this touch that makes Sherwood in this play seem more Continental than Molnar. It must be noted that Rudolf is not anxious to destroy Elena's marriage; he accepts facts as they are. He merely wishes to relive a past moment. He tells Elena, "But with me, it isn't as it would be with any one else. Can't you see that? I loved you first. And you loved me. You weren't lying when you said you loved me. You never knew how to lie. And I'm only asking you to love me again, for a little while, reminiscently, not as a rival of your husband, but as the echo of a voice that enchanted you when you were innocent and impressionable and young" (139).

When Anton and Rudolf finally meet in act three, they are completely civilized with each other and a friendship grows rapidly between them. But Anton's attitude is most revealing here. He offers to aid Rudolf in leaving Austria; but, in order to make arrangements for him to do this, he must leave Rudolf and Elena alone for the night. By this time Anton would be a rather unperceptive psychiatrist if he did not know what his absence would lead to. But he is for a moment sufficiently in awe of Rudolf that he turns his back on the situation and leaves the two former lovers together almost as a medieval peasant might have left his bride with the lord of the manor on his wedding night. Anton's reaction to Rudolf is very subtly presented, and it can be realized only in view of the emphasis which Sherwood places upon old Krug's reaction to Rudolf at breakfast the next morning. The father's awe is much more obvious than the son's but the one mirrors the other. The breakfast scene also contains a subtle representation of Sherwood's conclusions regarding the larger social concerns of the play. Anton has not yet returned home; however, his breakfast of kidneys has been cooked and awaits him. Old Krug would like to have kidneys for breakfast, but in this household such a delicacy is reserved for the Herr Professor. When Rudolf reaches for the kidneys, old Krug makes a feeble protest, but Rudolf pays no attention and takes that which is reserved for Anton. For anyone in the audience who could not tell by Miss Fontanne's expression what had transpired the night before, the answer is now given quite clearly.

The audience is also shown that sentimentality has triumphed, but that the triumph is temporary, for Rudolf must soon leave, never to return. And as a final bit of commentary, Sherwood has Elena say, "All the kidneys are gone . . . I'll tell Kathie to cook some more" (204). Had Rudolf not already been whisked away, he might have retorted, "What an obscene suggestion!" But Rudolph's words just before he is whisked away give the final Continental touch to this notably sophisticated comedy. He tells Anton, "I commend her to you—and you to her. It is a remarkable union, and it will give me satisfaction to the end of my days to think that perhaps I, in my small way, have contributed something to it" (202). This ending is clearly the same as the ending of *The Road to Rome* in which Hannibal says, "Fabius, I wish happiness and prosperity to you, your wife, and your sons." Fabius replies that he has no sons, to which Hannibal answers, "You may have" (*ed. cit.*, 176); and Hannibal presumably is in a better position to know than is Fabius. There is the suggestion in Rudolf's parting words that there are more Hapsburgs in Vienna than one can possibly imagine.

Reunion in Vienna, conceived in the leisure of two and a half years, was written hastily in three weeks. Sherwood's best plays were the result of hasty writing; intensity was a *sine qua non* in the literary production of the author. Yet, despite his haste in composition, Sherwood's plays had a finished quality about them which led Lawrence Langner to comment that ". . . with the exception of Eugene O'Neill, I know of no other playwright who produces a manuscript which, on first reading, is so ready for production."[6] Sherwood was always open to suggestion, but he did not appreciate being forced to haggle over petty criticism. *Reunion in Vienna* was his first Theatre Guild production, and one of the members of the Guild Board became much concerned with the psychological authenticity of Anton Krug. Sherwood wearied of this argument as it continued; and, largely as a result of it, he became disenchanted with the Guild's Board system. It was partly in rebellion against this system that he was to be co-founder along with Elmer Rice, Maxwell Anderson, and S. N. Behrman of the Playwrights' Producing Company.

There was virtually no adverse criticism of *Reunion in Vienna*. However, much of the criticism treated the acting more fully than the writing, and there was an over-all critical tendency to take the *play* for granted. Some critics made the unfortunate mistake of trying to judge this Continental comedy in terms of Iowa standards of morality, and the result was that sight was completely lost of what Sherwood was attempting. He was not concerned with condoning adultery as one notable critic presumed;[7] he was merely presenting a sentimental drama dealing with the shifting and uncertain values in a country which was changing from monarchy to republic.

The upholders of public morality in Toronto were to engage in a prolonged fray regarding *Reunion in Vienna*. Police intervention halted the production. No one denied the artistry of the play, but the level of criticism was essentially similar to that of John Coburn who called the production ". . . a parade of vice and falsehood . . . clothed in beautiful language, and presented with superb artistry."[8] The objections on the parts of New York critics were mild compared with those of some of the Canadian writers who reviewed the play. Essentially, the New Yorkers called upon Sherwood to do nothing more than alter fact: Mr. Skinner suggested that Sherwood could have given a satirical edge to his play by crushing the hollow romance which clings to the old empire. But, in making this suggestion,

Mr. Skinner reveals that he has little understanding of Vienna and of the Viennese.

It cannot be honestly said that *Reunion in Vienna* has a very original theme or that its development is very original. But the undeniable charm of the play places it many levels above most plays which have dealt with similar topics in a comic way. And in Sherwood's comedy there is a sadness at the passing of something about which people can feel the sort of sentiment which Sherwood saw in the Viennese. Willard Thorp demonstrated his understanding of the play when he wrote of it: "The mummeries of Rudolf's shabby court during its night of escape into the past represent one way in which modern man confronts the black doubt before him."[9] Sherwood's escape in this play did not represent a running away from reality but rather a standing still—an attempt to see in reality something less horrible than that which first appears.

CHAPTER 6

What Ever Happened to Brighton Perry?

"The dilemma of all writers, young and old, is in reconciling those problems of the human heart with a world state of mind that appears to become increasingly inhuman."
— From Sherwood's address, "Of Durability," delivered at the National Book Awards Banquet in 1951.

BEFORE ROBERT SHERWOOD was graduated from Milton Academy in 1914, he had begun to write pieces for publication. By the time he had finished his first semester at Harvard some of his work had been published in *Vanity Fair* both under his own name and under the pseudonym Brighton Perry. Sherwood was to continue writing almost until his death in November, 1955. In a period of some four decades, he established his name among the notables in the American theater as a playwright and as a moving force behind the Playwrights' Producing Company and the American National Theatre and Academy. He produced the enormous work entitled *Roosevelt and Hopkins* which *Time Magazine* called ". . . the best book on World War II by an American."[1] He wrote some of President Roosevelt's most stirring speeches and was generally to gain the reputation of being a thoroughly distinguished man of letters. However, despite the eminence which Sherwood gained, there are few critics who would call him a truly great figure in American theater; the statures of Eugene O'Neill, Tennessee Williams, Arthur Miller, and William Inge overshadow that of Robert Sherwood. But Sherwood was an engaging and urbane playwright. More

[142]

than half of his plays were excellent theater and were received warmly by audiences. Even his less successful early plays had about them a suggestion that the author was gaining mastery over his technique, and such imperfect works as *The Queen's Husband* and *Waterloo Bridge* were relatively well received.

Although Sherwood was not politically to the left, it is clearly apparent that his sympathies were essentially liberal and that Rooseveltian democracy was the political philosophy with which he felt most in harmony. Sherwood's liberal temperament and his high idealism found expression in a body of creative work which was notably romantic in character.[2] His romanticism comes full circle with *Small War on Murray Hill* in which the solution to the basic conflict is arrived at through purely romantic means, albeit the means are much more pedestrianly romantic than they had been in *The Road to Rome*.

Sherwood's romanticism is ill-defined and misdirected in such plays as *The Petrified Forest* and *Idiot's Delight*. The romantic, idealistic characters in these plays—Alan Squier, Quillery, Harry Van—make meaningless sacrifices; their sacrifices offer little hope of benefiting society. However, the romantic treatment of the Lincoln story in *Abe Lincoln in Illinois* has direction, as has the romantic idealism of Kaarlo Valkonen in *There Shall Be No Night*. Even Morey Vinion in the seriously defective drama *The Rugged Path* has a more clear-cut romantic idealism than have many earlier Sherwood protagonists.

Sherwood's most apparent and significant idea is the continuing and developing theme of pacifism which pervades all of his writing in one way or another. *The Road to Rome* is a statement of absolute pacifism under any circumstances, and this attitude is to be noted in all of Sherwood's works up to and including *Idiot's Delight*. However, with *Abe Lincoln in Illinois* Sherwood's pacifism becomes more moderate than it had been; and *Abe Lincoln in Illinois* leads directly into *There Shall Be No Night* in which the theory of peace at any cost is replaced by the one that freedom must be preserved even if its preservation necessarily involves its defenders in war. By the time Sherwood came to write *The Rugged Path*, he was willing to justify the idealist's going to war and dying for the cause of freedom. Unfortunately, Sherwood's loftier message in *The Rugged Path* is vitiated and obscured by the fact that Morey Vinion is escaping into war; he leaves behind him an intolerable situation and war gives him the opportunity to regain the individuality that a bourgeois society has seriously threatened to deprive him of. Sherwood permits his protagonist in this play to lose sight of the ideal which initially motivates him.

Sherwood was accused of doing an about face when he wrote *There Shall Be No Night*. Some pacifists for whom he had once been an eloquent spokesman now considered him a warmonger who had utterly deserted his former ideals.[3] However, it must be remembered that Sherwood's pacifism was always moral rather than political and that his whole reaction to the rise of the Axis powers was predicated more on basic morality than on political considerations. And Sherwood certainly was not alone in his reaction to the world crisis precipitated when the Germans attempted to seize much of Europe in 1939 and 1940. During this period, pacifist thought declined so markedly that the bulk of the American populace began to look upon pacifism as a form of treason.

This brings us to another point which must be made in any chapter containing conclusions about Sherwood: as an author, Sherwood was never really ahead of his time. He sensed the sentiments of the liberal, intelligent segment of American society and his plays were generally in complete accord with these sentiments at a given time. Sherwood did not purposely set out to mirror the philosophy and reactions of his society; however, his thinking was never revolutionary. It gave American intellectuals reassurance; it corroborated their deepest sentiments. Sherwood's plays gave utterance to what his audiences had been thinking, but they did not generally cause audiences to think in a new dimension. Audiences would nod in assent to the philosophy of Sherwood's plays, but they would not be led to action by it.

A significant part of Sherwood's philosophy is that personal sacrifice is necessary for the common good. Every Sherwood protagonist voluntarily makes a personal sacrifice through which Sherwood demonstrates his protagonist's human worth. And every selfless act performed by a protagonist is an eloquent pronouncement that the performer of the act is reaffirming his faith in humanity. Sherwood seems throughout his career to have been motivated by the Jungian principle which he finally states in *There Shall Be No Night*: "There is no coming to consciousness without pain."

Sherwood generally looked upon patriotism as a constricting and artificial force. He was essentially too broad in his thinking to write for narrowly patriotic ends. However, Sherwood's attitude toward patriotism is narrower in *Abe Lincoln in Illinois* than in his other plays. In *There Shall Be No Night*, he returns to a much broader code of loyalty; Dr. Valkonen is fighting for human freedom, not merely for Finland.

Willard Thorp has written that ". . . What was consistent in Sherwood's career was his unrelenting search for answers."[4] In a sense this is probably what accounts for some of his failures. When the search for answers was made secondary, as it was in *Reunion in Vienna*, the dramatic result was excellent. Both *The Petrified Forest* and *Idiot's Delight* would have benefited significantly from less introspection. By their natures *Abe Lincoln in Illinois* and *There Shall Be No Night* are well suited to the search for answers, but again in *The Rugged Path* and in *Small War on Murray Hill*, dramatic impact is sacrificed to philosophical searching.

Sherwood certainly spoke for himself, but hopefully not for all American dramatists, when he addressed the International Congress of Poets, Playwrights, Editors, Essayists, and Novelists in 1950: "Every writer is at heart a reformer, and if he knows that reformation is desperately needed, and it is not taking place, he feels a sense of personal guilt."[5] In Sherwood's case, the feeling was more one of responsibility than guilt; but his feeling of responsibility led him too often to soliloquized preachments. His urbanity was present in every play which he wrote, as was his graceful wit. However, his greatest artistic contributions were made when he allowed his wit to triumph over his sense of philosophical responsibility as he did in *The Road to Rome* and in *Reunion in Vienna*. Sherwood was a master of high comedy. Brilliant flashes of comedy exist in *The Road to Rome*, and the culmination of Sherwood's comedy comes, of course, in *Reunion in Vienna*. Even such inferior pieces as *The Queen's Husband* and *This Is New York* have in them moments of exceptional wit.

It would not be honest or fair to contend that Sherwood achieved literary greatness of historic proportions. The author himself realized what his shortcomings were. However, Sherwood's greatest strength was in his warm and genuine humanity, a humanity which made baseness, crassness, and brutality completely inimical to him. Sherwood loved mankind and this love was reciprocated by those who knew him. He was a man with virtually no enemies. Even in the company of the sophisticates of the Hotel Algonquin, which he frequented when it was a small and select literary mecca, Sherwood was able to remain the friend of members of the most antipodal factions. His encompassing humanity touched all who had contact with him and made them better people. His plays, for the most part works which demonstrate a high degree of competence, reflect his warm humanity and his genuine concern for mankind. American theater is stronger because Robert Emmet Sherwood was integrally a part of it during the crucial years in its struggle toward identity.

Notes and References

Chapter One

1. John Gassner, "Robert Emmet Sherwood," *Atlantic Monthly*, CLXIX (1942), 26.
2. S. N. Behrman, "Old Monotonous," *New Yorker*, XVI (June 8, 1940), 28.
3. *Waterloo Bridge* (New York, 1930), pp. xix-xx.
4. "Do You Like the Talkies? Yes," *The Golden Book*, XI (April, 1930), 52.
5. *Ibid.*
6. "Renaissance in Hollywood," *American Mercury*, XVI (1929), 437.
7. "Beyond the Talkies—Television," *Scribner's Magazine*, LXXXVI, 8.
8. Eleanor Flexner, *American Playwrights, 1918-1938*, p. 273.
9. *Catholic World*, CXXXIV (1931-32), 468.
10. *Time Magazine*, XXVII (April 6, 1936), 38.
11. *American Playwrights, 1918-1938*, p. 272.
12. Dowager Queen of Rumania from 1927 until her death in 1938. Author of several books in English, among them *My Country* (1916) *Ilderim* (1925), *The Story of My Life* (1934-35), and *The Mask* (1935). Married Ferdinand, who became King.
13. Published in *Saturday Review of Literature*, IX (March 4, 1933), 161-62.
14. For additional data see "What OWI Is Doing," by Elmer Davis, *Saturday Review of Literature*, XXV (December 5, 1942), 9; "Information Please," *Life*, XIII (July 27, 1942), 37-39; "U. S. Propaganda," *Time Magazine*, XL (October 12, 1945), 44, 46.
15. "Easing In," *Time Magazine*, LXIII (January 4, 1954), 40.
16. *Saturday Review*, XXXVII (January 16, 1954), 34.

Chapter Two

1. See, for example, Richard Jennings' review of the play in *Spectator*, CXL (1928), 826-27.
2. "Footnote to a Preface," *Saturday Review of Literature*, XXXII (August 6, 1949), 130. See also Roger M. Busfield, Jr., *The Playwright's Art*, p. 159.

3. *Illustrated News* (London), CLXXII (1928), 996.

4. Note Stark Young's incisive comments in his review of the play, *New Republic*, L (March 9, 1927), 70-71.

5. *There Shall Be No Night* (New York, 1940), pp.xii-xiii.

6. *American Playwrights, 1918-1938*, p. 273.

7. S. N. Behrman, "Old Monotonous," *New Yorker*, XVI (June 1, 1940), 36.

8. Flexner, *op. cit.*, p. 274.

9. *Theory and Technique of Playwriting*, pp. 262-67.

10. "The Road to Inclenberg [*sic*] Heights," *Saturday Review*, XL (January 19, 1957), 48.

11. *Catholic World*, CLXXXIV (1957), 471.

12. LXIX (January 14, 1957), 68.

13. "Two Minor Skirmishes," *New Yorker*, XXXII (January 12, 1957), 58.

14. *Ibid.*

Chapter Three

1. *Time Magazine*, XXVII (May 11, 1936), 50. See also Henry Seidel Canby, "The Pulitzer Prize Winners," *Saturday Review of Literature*, XIV (May 9, 1936), 6-7. Mr. Canby writes, ". . . there is a rapturous shout when the drama prize is given to Robert E. Sherwood for his anti-war play, *Idiot's Delight*."

2. *The Road to Rome*, ed. cit., p. 42.

3. See, for example, Euphemia van Rensselear Wyatt's review of the play, *Catholic World*, CXXXII (1930-31), 464.

4. For a general outline of dramatic structure see John Howard Lawson, *op. cit.*, pp. 221-302.

5. *Bookman*, LXXII (1931), 516.

6. *Outlook and Independent*, CLVI (1930), 629.

7. Joseph Wood Krutch, "Heartbreak House," *Nation*, CXL (January 23, 1935), 111.

8. Lawson, *op. cit.*, p. 143.

9. *Ibid.*

10. *Ibid.*

11. "The Play," *Commonweal*, XXI (1935), 375.

12. "Particular and General," *New Republic*, LXXXII (February 13, 1935), 21.

13. CXIX (January 19, 1935), 19.

14. *Ibid.*, 22.

15. *Catholic World*, CXL (1934-35), 601.

16. Brian Doherty, "Footlights," *Canadian Forum*, XV (1934-35), 194.

17. *The Road to Rome, ed. cit.,* p. 121.

18. *Famous American Plays of the 1930's,* pp. 12-13.

19. *Ibid.,* p. 13.

20. Casper Nannes, *Politics in the American Drama* (Washington, 1960), pp. 153-54, 224.

21. *Broadway in Review,* p. 156.

22. S. N. Behrman, "Old Monotonous," *New Yorker,* XVI (June 1, 1940), 36.

23. Harold Clurman, *op. cit.,* pp. 13-14.

24. Lawrence Langner, *The Magic Curtain,* pp. 265-66.

25. XXIII (1936), 664.

26. *Ibid.,* XXIV (1936), 104.

27. *Newsweek,* VII (April 4, 1936), 32.

28. *Commonweal,* XXIII (1936), 664.

29. *John Gassner,* "Robert Emmet Sherwood," *Atlantic Monthly,* CLXIX (January, 1942), 31.

30. "The Devil's Time," *Nation,* CXLII (April 5, 1936), 491.

Chapter Four

1. "Magdalene," *Nation,* CXXX (1930), 106.

2. "Mostly the Actors," *New Republic,* LXI (1930), 251.

3. Paul C. Harris, Jr., *The Relation of Dramatic Structure to the Ideas in Robert E. Sherwood's Dramatic Works.* Unpublished Ph.D. Dissertation (Stanford University, 1959), p. 305.

4. *The Cycle of American Literature* (Mentor Edition), p. 193.

5. *Idiot's Delight, ed. cit.,* p. 189.

6. Harris, *op. cit.,* p. 306.

7. *Broadway in Review,* p. 152.

8. *Ibid.*

9. *Supra,* 64-65.

10. John Howard Lawson, *The Theory and Technique of Playwriting* (New York, 1960), pp. 142-46.

11. *The American Drama Since 1918,* p. 316.

12. *Commonweal,* XXX (1939), 526.

13. *Nation,* CLX (1945), 562.

14. XXXV (May 13, 1940), 52.

15. Lawrence Langner, *The Magic Curtain,* pp. 328-29.

16. *Commonweal,* XXXII (May 10, 1940), 62.

17. "The Riddle of the Sphinx," *Nation,* CL (1940), 605-6.

18. Nannes, *op. cit.,* p. 156.

19. Washington *Evening Star,* May 11, 1940, p. F1.

20. *Broadway in Review,* p. 156.

21. *Ibid.*, p. 157.
22. *Theatre Arts Monthly*, XXIV (June, 1940), 399.
23. Paul Charles Harris, Jr., *op. cit.*, p. 308.
24. Burns Mantle, *The Best Plays of 1945-46*, p. 308.
25. New York *Times*, November 15, 1945, p. 25.
26. XLVI (November 19, 1945), 63.
27. *Ibid.*, p. 64.
28. *Nation*, CLXI (November 24, 1945), 562.
29. *Commonweal*, XLIII (November 30, 1945), 168.
30. Paul Charles Harris, Jr., *op. cit.*, p. 312.
31. *The Queen's Husband*, p. xvi.
32. *Outlook*, CLIX (September 2, 1931), 1, 26.
33. New York *Times Book Review*, September 13, 1931, p. 20.

Chapter Five

1. *American Writing in the Twentieth Century*, p. 94.
2. Francis R. Bellamy, "Lights Down," *Outlook*, CXLVIII (1928), 235.
3. XXXIV (1928), 351.
4. *Ibid.*
5. *The American Drama Since 1918*, p. 216. See also Krutch's review, "Sham Battle of the Sexes," *Nation*, CXXXIII (1931), 650-51.
6. *The Magic Curtain*, p. 253.
7. Richard Dana Skinner, "The Play," *Commonweal*, XV (1931), p. 160.
8. *Canadian Forum*, XIV (1933-34), 367. See also N. L. Dale's retort to Coburn's comments. *Ibid.*, 410-11, and Maurice Colbourne's review of the police intervention in his article "Mittens and Mud," *Ibid.*, 300-1.
9. *American Writing in the Twentieth Century*, p. 94.

Chapter Six

1. LII (November 15, 1948), 110.
2. Of the established critics who have written on Sherwood, only Alan S. Downer considers him a realist, and Downer's claim in this case is not very convincingly supported or illustrated. For his contentions see *Fifty Years of American Drama* (Chicago, 1951), p. 92.
3. See *Time Magazine*, XXXV (May 13, 1940), 52, for Sherwood's reaction to the accusation that he was advocating intervention.
4. *American Writing in the Twentieth Century*, p. 93.
5. *Saturday Review of Literature*, XXXIII (October 21, 1950), 22.

Selected Bibliography

PRIMARY SOURCES

1. *Major Works*

Abe Lincoln in Illinois. New York: Charles Scribner's Sons, 1939.

Idiot's Delight. New York: Charles Scribner's Sons, 1936.

The Petrified Forest. New York: Charles Scribner's Sons, 1935.

The Queen's Husband. New York: Charles Scribner's Sons, 1928.

Reunion in Vienna. New York: Charles Scribner's Sons, 1932.

Roosevelt and Hopkins, An Intimate History. New York: Harper, 1948; enlarged and revised, 1950. The British edition was entitled *The White House Papers of Harry L. Hopkins, An Intimate History* and was published in London by Eyre and Spottiswoode, 1949, in two volumes.

The Rugged Path. Burns Mantle, ed. *Best Plays of 1945-46.* New York: Dodd, Mead and Company, Inc., 1946. This is the only printed version of the play.

Small War on Murray Hill. New York: Dramatists' Play Service, 1957.

There Shall Be No Night. New York: Charles Scribner's Sons, 1940.

This Is New York. New York: Charles Scribner's Sons, 1931.

Virtuous Knight. New York: Charles Scribner's Sons, 1931.

Waterloo Bridge. New York: Charles Scribner's Sons, 1930.

2. *Miscellaneous Works*

The Best Years of Our Lives: How a Film Is Made. Hollywood: [1946].

The Free Company Presents . . . An American Crusade. New York: Dodd, Mead and Company, 1941.

Hold Everything! New York: Sherwood's [1929].

How to Write and Sell Film Stories by Frances Marion. New York: Covici-Friede [1937], contains a shooting script of Sherwood's *Marco Polo.*

Second Threshold by Philip Barry. Completed, revised, and with an introduction by Robert E. Sherwood, New York: Harper, 1951.

Tovarich by Jacques Deval. Translated and adapted by Robert E. Sherwood. New York: Charles Scribner's Sons, 1937.

Unending Crusade. London: Heinemann, 1932.

3. *Articles*

Because Sherwood wrote so prodigiously for periodicals, it is necessary to present a selected bibliography of this phase of his work. The twenty-five items listed below represent a cross-section of his writing and give some indication of the broad scope of his interests.

"Beyond the Talkies, Television," *Scribner's,* LXXXVI (July, 1929), 1-8.

"The Big Stone Book," *American Heritage,* V (Winter, 1953-54), 3-5.

"Credo," *Survey,* LXXXVII (March, 1951), 118.

"Do You Like the Talkies? Yes," *Golden Book,* XI (April, 1930), 53.

"The Dramatic Life of Abraham Lincoln," *Life,* February 14, 1924, p. 24.

"The Dwelling Place of Wonder," *Theatre Arts Anthology,* Rosamond Gilder, ed. New York: Theatre Arts Books (1950), pp. 1-4.

"Elmer Davis in a Former Life," *New Republic,* CXXX (1954), 12.

"Extra! Extra!" *Golden Book,* XI (January, 1930), 19-23.

"Footnote to a Preface," *Saturday Review of Literature,* XXXII (August 6, 1949), 130ff.

"Harry Hopkins," *New Republic,* CXIV (1946), 180-81.

"He Was a Political Genius" [On Roosevelt], *New Republic,* CXIV (1946), 537-38.

"Inaugural Parade," *Saturday Review of Literature,* IX (March 4, 1933), 461-62.

"It's Only Funny Once," *Rotarian,* XLIX (September, 1936), 20-22.

"Jim Crow in Washington," *New Republic,* CXV (1946), 623.

"Letter to the Editor," *Golden Book,* XI (1930), 20.

"Letter to the Editor," New York *Times,* April 15, 1934, Section X, p. 2.

"Most Terrible Drama of All Time," *Saturday Review of Literature,* XXXIII (October 21, 1950), 22-23.

"Of Durability," *Saturday Review of Literature,* XXXIV (March 17, 1951), 22.

"Please Don't Frighten Us," *Atlantic Monthly,* CLXXXVII (February, 1949), 79.

"Renaissance in Hollywood," *American Mercury,* XVI (1929), 431-37.

"Romance in Purple," *Pictorial Review,* XXXII (November, 1930), 1.

"There Is No Alternative to Peace," *Fortune,* LII (July, 1955), 84ff.

"To Summer—and Return," New York *Times,* March 19, 1939, Section XI, p. 2.

"The Vanishing American Playwright," *Saturday Review of Literature,* XXIII (February 1, 1941), 12.

"The War We Do Not Want." *Collier's,* CXXVIII (October 27, 1951), 19-31ff.

SECONDARY SOURCES

1. *Books*

Although no full-length studies of Robert Emmet Sherwood have yet been published, the following books contain pertinent information regarding his life and works. Soon to be published is an authoritative biography of Sherwood by his close friend and associate, John Mason Brown.

BLOCK, ANITA. *The Changing World in Plays and Theatre.* Boston: Little, Brown and Company, 1939. Although she does not deal specifically with Sherwood in her book, Miss Block's presentation of the temper of the theater-going public during the 1930's is helpful in understanding Sherwood's popular success.

BROWN, JOHN MASON. *Two on the Aisle.* New York: W. W. Norton and Company, 1938. Brown probes beneath the comedy of *Idiot's Delight* and the melodrama of *The Petrified Forest* to bare the allegorical core of both works.

DOWNER, ALAN S. *Fifty Years of American Drama.* Chicago: Henry Regnery Co., 1951. Although Downer is unconvincing in his statement that Sherwood is a realist whose realism ranks with that of O'Neill, Barry, and Howard, his comments on *Abe Lincoln in Illinois* are illuminating.

DUSENBURY, WINIFRED L. *The Theme of Loneliness in Modern American Drama.* Gainesville: University of Florida Press, 1960. This study is especially valuable for its penetrating insights into *Abe Lincoln in Illinois.* The author's comments on *Idiot's Delight, The Petrified Forest,* and *The Rugged Path* are provocative.

FLEXNER, ELEANOR. *American Playwrights: 1918-1938.* New York: Simon and Schuster, 1938. Miss Flexner deals with Sherwood's development through *Idiot's Delight* and provides especially sensitive commentary on *The Petrified Forest* and *Idiot's Delight.*

GAGEY, EDMOND M. *Il Teatro in America: 1900-1950.* Rome: Edizioni di Storia e Letteratura, 1954. Gagey emphasizes Sherwood's romanticism and is especially strong in relating *Abe Lincoln in Illinois* to other Lincoln plays such as Emma Goodman's *If Booth Had Missed,* John Drinkwater's *Abraham Lincoln,* and E. P. Conkle's *Prologue to Glory.* Comments also on Sherwood's extreme loyalty to the principles of the New Deal.

GASSNER, JOHN. *Theatre at the Crossroads.* New York: Holt, Rinehart and Winston, 1960. Gassner considers Sherwood not only a master comedian, but also a polished exemplar of dramatic journalism.

KRUTCH, JOSEPH WOOD. *The American Drama Since 1918: An Informal*

History. New York: Random House, 1939. Mr. Krutch writes with his usual verve and insight, but his consideration of Sherwood in a chapter dealing exclusively with comedy tends to limit his view of the author's works through *Idiot's Delight*.

LAWSON, JOHN HOWARD. *Theory and Technique of Playwriting*. New York: G. P. Putnam's Sons, 1936. Republished, New York: Hill and Wang, 1960. This is by far the most adequate discussion in print of the dramatic techniques used by Sherwood in *The Petrified Forest*. It is an extraordinarily valuable study in depth of this play from a purely technical point of view.

MANTLE, BURNS. *American Playwrights of Today*. New York: Dodd, Mead and Company, 1929. This is one of the earliest appraisals of Sherwood as a major playwright.

MERSAND, JOSEPH. *American Drama Goes to War*. New York: Modern Chapbooks, 1943. The last chapter, "American Dramatists and the Axis," deals with *Idiot's Delight* and *There Shall Be No Night*.

————. *The American Drama, 1930-40*. New York: Modern Chapbooks, 1941. Mersand relates *Abe Lincoln in Illinois* to other Lincoln plays such as Gagey later did in his book mentioned above.

NANNES, CASPER. *Politics in the American Drama as Revealed by Plays Produced on the New York Stage, 1890-1945*. Philadelphia: University of Pennsylvania Press, 1950. Republished as *Politics in the American Drama*, Washington: Catholic University of America Press, 1960. This study is valuable in establishing the fact that Sherwood's pacifism was moral rather than political.

O'HARA, FRANK HURBURT. *Today in American Drama*. Chicago: University of Chicago Press, 1939. Especially helpful to the Sherwood scholar are O'Hara's comments on *Abe Lincoln in Illinois* in Chapter II, "Comedies without Laughter."

THORP, WILLARD. *American Writing in the Twentieth Century*. Cambridge: Harvard University Press, 1960. Chapter III, "Dramatic Interlude, 1915-1940," is especially relevant to the student of Sherwood. Thorp considers Sherwood a writer of high comedy. He notes Sherwood's profound interest in the issues of his time and comments that in his plays he was always searching for answers.

2. *Unpublished studies*

HARRIS, PAUL CHARLES. *The Relation of Dramatic Structure to the Ideas in Robert E. Sherwood's Dramatic Works*. Unpublished doctoral dissertation, Stanford University, 1959. This study is the fullest extant consideration of Robert Sherwood's dramas. Harris' tracing of Sherwood's pacifist thought is very well handled.

HOSTETTER, PAUL SMITH. *A Production Book of Robert E. Sherwood's* THE PETRIFIED FOREST. Unpublished master's thesis, Stanford University, 1949. This study contains a strong introductory overview of Sherwood's life and works and presents a well-annotated script of *The Petrified Forest.*

PENROD, JOHN A. *American Literature and the Great Depression.* Unpublished doctoral dissertation, University of Pennsylvania, 1954. Penrod considers Sherwood to be little concerned with the problems of the Depression except in *The Petrified Forest* where only a minimum of the era's problems is presented.

SCANLAN, ROSS. *Drama as a Form of Persuasive Communication.* Unpublished doctoral dissertation, Cornell University, 1937. Scanlan considers the subtle persuasive power of *The Road to Rome, The Petrified Forest,* and *Idiot's Delight.*

3. *Articles in periodicals*

Sherwood's plays from *Reunion in Vienna* to *Small War on Murray Hill* were extensively reviewed in periodical literature. The most satisfactory and reliable reviews were generally found in *Commonweal, Nation, New Republic, Newsweek, Saturday Review of Literature, Theatre Arts Monthly,* and *Time.* Because of the large number of reviews available for each of Sherwood's plays, individual reviews are not referred to here. Rather articles of a more general biographical or critical nature are included.

ATKINSON, BROOKS. "Bob Sherwood," New York *Times,* January 13, 1957, Section II, p. 1. A brief but sound over-all estimate of Sherwood on the occasion of the posthumous production of *Small War on Murray Hill.*

————. "Double Play, Lardner to Sherwood," New York *Times,* December 23, 1927, p. 17. An early consideration of Sherwood and one of the few reviews of *The Love Nest.*

BEHRMAN, S. N. "Old Monotonous," *New Yorker,* XVI (June 1 and June 8, 1940), 33-40, 26-33. Well-written, witty presentation of Sherwood's development up to *There Shall Be No Night.* A most helpful presentation of Sherwood's background and of his stature as dramatist.

"Easing In," *Time Magazine,* LXIII (January 4, 1954), 40. This brief article tells of Sherwood's emergence as a writer for television.

GASSNER, JOHN. "Robert Emmett Sherwood," *Atlantic Monthly,* CLXIX (1942), 26-33. Similar in nature to Behrman's article,

Gassner's consideration does more to present Sherwood in a critical rather than a biographical light. A necessary and thoughtful supplement to Behrman's excellent article.

ISAACS, EDITH. "Robert Sherwood," *Theatre Arts Monthly*, XXIII (1939), 31-40. A good consideration of the growth of Sherwood's romanticism and of the course which his pacifism followed. Comments on his use of language and on his capturing of the rhythms of speech.

RICE, ELMER. "A Personal Memoir," New York *Times*, November 30, 1955, Section II, pp. 1-3. An appreciative reminiscence occasioned by Sherwood's death two weeks earlier. Insights into Sherwood's activities in theatrical organizations such as the Playwrights' Producing Company.

SMITH, COLLIE. "Robert Sherwood—King of English," *Collier's*, CXXII (April 30, 1949), 70. A consideration of Sherwood as writer and especially of his use of the language. This article is at a popular level, but provides some perceptive insights.

SMITH, HARRISON. "Robert E. Sherwood," *Saturday Review of Literature*, XXXVIII (November 26, 1955), 24, 31. A biographical resumé and an appreciation written two weeks after Sherwood's death.

"U. S. Propaganda," *Time Magazine*, XL (October 12, 1945), 44, 46. Concerned with Sherwood's position as director of the Overseas Branch of the Office of War Information.

"The War Nobody Liked," *Time Magazine*, LIX (January 14, 1952), 56. An interesting article on the reception of the publication of "The War We Do Not Want," to which Sherwood was a significant contributor, by *Collier's*. Sherwood withdrew his part of the series from Simon and Schuster who planned to publish it in book form.

WOOLF, S. J. "A Playwright Enlists in the War of Ideas," New York *Times Magazine*, July 7, 1940, p. 8. This is more than just another review of *There Shall Be No Night*. It is a thoughtful consideration of Sherwood's dramatic and philosophic growth.

Index

Index